How to Use Camping Experiences in Religious Education

Dedicated to Cindy—who, in believing in what she could not see, saw more in me than I ever thought possible. —Steve

KENOSIS SERIES

How to Use Camping Experiences in Religious Education

Kenosis is a venerable biblical term (Phil 2:7) which orthodox Patristic exegetes interpreted as expressing the process whereby the Second Person of the Trinity emptied himself into history and took on human form. In the ongoing kenotic process, Jesus fully had two distinct but united human natures, God and human. This hypostatic union always remains and can never be dissolved. In this kenotic process, the human nature of Jesus was directly and immediately sanctified by his intimate contact with his fully-functioning though usually hidden divine nature. In the kenosis, Jesus typically subjected his divine nature to the total service of his human nature in order in order to accomplish the two basic purposes in God's overall eschatological design: redemption and religious instruction.

Each Kenosis Book is analogous in some ways to the biblical kenosis. In the pedagogical kenosis, inexhaustible theory empties itself into the religious instruction act and takes on practical form. In this pedagogical kenosis, the religious instruction act has two distinct but interactive natures, theory and practice. This union always remains and can never be dissolved. In the kenotic process, the practice nature of the religious instruction act is directly and immediately made fruitful by its intimate contact with the usually hidden theoretical nature. In the pedagogical kenosis, the religious instruction act subjects its theoretical dimension to the total service of practice in order to effectively achieve desired religious instruction outcomes.

How to Use Camping Experiences in Religious Education: Transformation through Christian Camping

by

Stephen F. Venable

and

Donald M. Joy

A Kenosis Book

Religious Education Press
Birmingham, Alabama

Library of Congress Cataloging-in-Publication Data

Venable, Stephen F., 1960–
    How to use camping experiences in religious education: transformation through Christian camping / by Stephen F. Venable and Donald M. Joy.
    p. cm. — (A kenosis book)
    Includes bibliographical references and index.
    ISBN 0-89135-104-3 (pbk.: alk. paper)
    1. Church camps.   I. Joy, Donald M. (Donald Marvin), 1928–   .
II. Title. III. Series.
BV1650.V38   1998   98-13828
268'.6—dc21   CIP

Religious Education Press
5316 Meadow Brook Road
Birmingham, Alabama 35242–3315
10 9 8 7 6 5 4 3 2

Religious Education Press publishes books exclusively in religious education and in areas closely related to religious education. It is committed to enhancing and professionalizing religious education through the publication of serious, significant, and scholarly works.

PUBLISHER TO THE PROFESSION

CONTENTS

WELCOME TO RELIGIOUS CAMPING LEADERSHIP: WHAT YOU WILL LEARN FROM READING THIS BOOK

In *How to Use Camping Experiences in Religious Education*, two veteran camp leaders, Steve Venable and Don Joy, offer you a walking tour of basic and effective religious camping principles. We share insights that are based on camping experience. Whether you are a professional or a novice, this handbook can help you run a religious camping program. We speak from our own experience and religious perspective, but the principles we offer apply to a wide spectrum of faith traditions.

How to Use Camping Experiences in Religious Education is designed to get you up and running as quickly as possible. Chapters 3–11 constitute the "handbook" tools, each offering information on a specific aspect of religious camping. Each chapter ends with an annotated bibliography that points the way to other resources.

Camping is an effective tool for bringing people to Christian faith and for nurturing and deepening discipleship. The very act of getting away from our normal routine and immersing ourselves in an intentionally religious setting of people and activities sets the stage for personal transformation. Camping is one important aspect of holistic religious education for children, youth, and adults.

Chapter 2 explains the history of religious camping—beginning with the Old Testament.

Chapter 3 deals with the power of community. Camping programs offer opportunities for community building that are not broadly available in communities and churches.

Chapter 4 focuses on the importance of Scripture study in various camp settings and offers hints on designing a Bible study.

Chapter 5 describes effective worship experiences for campers, and offers practical implementation guidelines.

Chapter 6 is about finding, recruiting, and training camp counselors—key members of your leadership team.

Chapter 7 examines rites of passage as tools for transformation and commitment. The religious camp offers a setting in which key life events can be orchestrated for campers.

Chapter 8 looks beyond the "same old" camp program and style and envisions new avenues for growth through camping.

Chapter 9 teaches you how to implement various types of camps, from planning to scheduling to budgeting.

Chapter 10 takes a close look at recruiting and empowering a leadership team for your camp.

Chapter 11 may be our favorite. Fixed-site camping professionals that we are, both of us have found the pilgrimage feature of backcountry camping to be uniquely an opportunity for *How to Use Camping Experiences in Religious Education*.

Chapter 12 recaps what you will experience as you read this book.

GETTING STARTED IN RELIGIOUS CAMPING

Many cultural and societal factors led to the rise of organized camping in the late 1800s, so it is difficult to separate "secular" from "religious" influences. For most of human history, individuals have "camped out" in some form or other as a way of life, but organized, purposeful camping is a relatively new concept with roots in American history. Eleanor Eells's *History of Organized Camping: The First One Hundred Years* is a definitive statement on the movement's roots and uniqueness. Most of the summary in this chapter follows her book.

HISTORY OF ORGANIZED AND RELIGIOUS CAMPING

By the late nineteenth century the west had been won. The Industrial Revolution was changing the shape of life for an increasing number of American families as people moved away from slow-paced, un-crowded rural life to fast-growing, often crowded areas that threw up new problems for families. As educational opportunities increased in this urban, industrial society, so did leisure time. A host of public institutions emerged to provide organized educational opportunities for young people in a society where they were largely ignored.

Around this time, Victorian intolerance for the natural and primitive gave way to a romantic interest in the common man and nature. Among the affluent, men and boys began to seek the experience of "roughing it" in the wild for a few days at a time. They regained a sense of adventure, of the old west coming alive once more. Women, traditionally bound to their domestic responsibilities, were also attracted to the adventure and renewal potential of intentional outdoor experiences.

Another factor in the rise of organized camping was the influence of Native Americans. Though they were feared and hated by some, others admired certain elements of their cultures, lifestyles, and traditions. Their symbiotic relationship with nature, as opposed to the conquering spirit of manifest destiny, was appealing to many. Even today many camps pass along outdoor living skills, songs, dances, names, and other traditions deeply rooted in Native traditions.

It was out of this cultural milieu that organized camping arose. Outdoor experiences seemed to serve to bring people together, instill trust, and generate a renewed sense of purpose. As men and women attempted to deal creatively with new social issues and problems, they laid the foundations of camping as a means for social and religious change.

Frederick William Gunn (1816–81) was headmaster at the Gunnery School in Connecticut. He organized frequent weekend trips into the woods as well as extensive hiking and sports year-round for the boys of his school. These activities were designed to strengthen the students' body and character. In August 1861, Gunn and his wife led the entire student body on a two-week trip at the end of the school year. They hiked forty miles to Welch's Point on Long Island Sound in two days. The idea was to live simply, as a soldier might, sharing the cooking and other chores. There were other similar excursions in the years that followed, including annual encampments at Lake Waramaug, seven miles from the school, through 1879.

The first person to establish an independent camp, separate from a school or other organization was Ernest Balch. While attending Dartmouth College, he had observed that teenage children were forced to accompany their parents to summer resorts where they came under the evil influence of high society. Camp Chocorua was built in May of 1881 on Burnt Island in Squam Lake, New Hampshire, to duplicate the carefree and natural conditions that Balch had experienced during his childhood. That summer five boys from Washington and Boston arrived for the first camp. Balch was reported to have exclaimed, "We had a camp! My ideas were sound." The camp grew throughout its eight years of existence, as Balch realized the dream of his life.

Balch was the first to bring religious concepts and influence to bear intentionally on organized camping. He was known for his missionary zeal and recruited boys mostly from Episcopal schools. Camp Chocorua had a hilltop chapel that grew with the camp, attracting worshipers from nearby towns to evening vespers. Balch also began acolyte and choir programs for his boys. Other devoted Christians to influence camping included Luther (1865–1918) and Charlotte (1865–1928) Gulick. The Gulicks, both children of missionaries, influenced the formation and goals of several camping programs through organizations such as the YMCA (Young Men's Christian Association) and Camp Fire girls. Though the Gulicks had once hoped to become foreign missionaries, they are now remembered as outstanding and innovative home missionaries, heralding the good news of organized camps as instruments of education for mind, soul, and body.

Reverend George Hinckley (1853–1950) is credited with founding the first church camp. He took four boys from his parish and three Chinese students who were being educated in the United States on a camping trip to Gardner's Island at Wakefield, Rhode Island, in 1880. He later organized the Good Will Farm for boys in Maine, from which the Good Will Encampment operated as an extension ministry.

By the 1950s, most denominations had established campsites, assembly grounds, and conference centers for ministry with youth and adults. Though many of these camps were at remote locations, they usually held nature at a distance. The experience of camping became increasingly centered around structures and increasingly removed from nature. But following decades saw a growing concern for environmental and back-to-nature issues, as well as a desire to develop relational competency. Religious camping responded by training directors and counselors in group dynamics and teaching them to be more intentionally theological and religious in their approach to the various elements of a camping program. The influence of decentralized camping, which placed participants in small groups instead of keeping them together as a single, much larger group, continued to grow. These smaller, more personal "families" facilitated stronger relationships between counselors and campers and led to greater personal growth in a shorter period of time.

A high-tech movement in the 1960s and 1970s spurred innovations and developments in every area from the space program to experimental theology and spiritual awakenings, and campers flocked to the outdoors in order to "experience" God through nature. The 1980s, however, saw a return to simplicity in campers' spiritual quests, and off-site and other nontraditional forms of camping began to grow in popularity. Many religious groups and camps began to use backpacking, canoeing, stresscamping, biking, and other outdoor living skills to develop campers.

The scriptural mandate to go out beyond the normal boundaries of our lives in search of God, or better yet, to be found by God, is embedded in the Exodus wilderness wanderings of the nation of Israel. God sent Moses to Pharaoh with this command: "Let my people go, so that they may hold a festival to me in the desert" (Ex 5:1 NIV). The Exodus story tells of a people being uprooted from their normal way of life to find the promises of God in an unknown and far-off place. Through the challenges laid before them in their "camping" experience, the Hebrew people were tested and tried in their forty-year search. In the Old Testament, the word "desert" or "wilderness" indicates a place where the Lord reveals himself. But it is also the abode of demons that threaten people with sickness and impurities. On their journey through this place, between who they were and who they were becoming, the Hebrews found out who God had indeed created them to be. And they were re-rooted in their Promised Land. Though an entire generation lost their lives in the wilderness because of their disobedience, it was also a place where God revealed himself through signs and wonders.

For Jesus, the wilderness was a place where no one lived, a special place where nothing separated him from God. "So He Himself often withdrew into the wilderness and prayed" (Lk 5:16 NKJV). He often fled the familiar people and places around him as he longed for a closer walk with God. Several times in Scripture God uses the wilderness (literally "solitary place") to create a solitary place in Jesus' life. During his threefold temptation by Satan in the wilderness, Jesus found power in the solitude of the wilderness. It could be said that his forty-day ordeal in the wilderness (Lk 4:1–13) was more for preparation for ministry than for temptation. At other times Jesus went to the wilderness with his closest followers. The reason was the same: to find a time and place to draw strength from God.

John the Baptist was also transformed by God in the wilderness. Luke writes that "he lived in the desert until he appeared publicly to Israel" (1:80 NIV). His calling was prophesied by Isaiah:

> A voice of one calling:
> "In the desert prepare
> the way for the LORD;
> make straight in the wilderness
> a highway for our God.
> Every valley shall be raised up,
> every mountain and hill made
> low;
> the rough ground shall become
> level,
> the rugged places a plain.
> And the glory of the LORD will be
> revealed,
> and all mankind together will
> see it.
> For the mouth of the LORD
> has spoken" (40:3–5 NIV).

The Baptist's "camping" experience produced the cauldron from which the fire of his message "preaching a baptism of repentance for the forgiveness of sins" (Lk 3:3 NIV) was formed. But he had to live it out in the community of the repentant. God did not leave John in the desert. God called him to use that experience, as well as the strength it gave him, to reach others and to change the lives of many (cf. Lk 7:25–28).

Bob Cagle writes in *Youth Ministry Camping* that the Greek word for incarnation, *skenoo*, usually translated "he dwelled among us," literally means "he tented with us." The experience of Christian camping is another opportunity for us to discover the reality of God with us, both in the wilderness and at home.

The wilderness, for all its solitude, is just the place to be after all. As singer/songwriter Michael Card says, wandering in the wilderness is "the best place to be found." For the Israelites, as well as for Jesus and John and all others who choose to go there in search of God, the "camping" experience was a credential for ministering in the power and the Spirit of the Lord.

TEACHING/LEARNING PRINCIPLES
UNDERLYING RELIGIOUS CAMPING

The principles offered here are based on solid evidence about how camping initiates change in participants. Piromrak Evans observed girls in a summer camp, using pre- and posttest self-concept measures. Evans documents a significant positive difference between the mean scores on the self-esteem of campers before and after the experience. On each of the five factors measured, as well as on total score, there were significant gains. In another study Linda Kay collected data on two six-day camping trips, completed pre- and posttest measures on moral reasoning, and collected ethnographic and other data in an effort to measure the impact of camping on the rehabilitation of young offenders. One group was male and the other was female. Kay found that postcamp recidivism was more positively reduced for boys than for girls. Campers showed self-identification beyond the label "delinquent" in direct proportion to their positive involvement during the week of camp life. Since the recommendations in this book focus on the potentials of specifically Christian-grounded camping, it is impressive that careful study of effects of religious-education based camping mark significant gains in spiritual wellness and in actual commitment to careers in ministry service.

There is hard evidence that Christian camping leads to predictable transformation. An exploratory study of a week-long Rocky Mountain backpacking trip conducted by Stephen Venable, measured "religious and existential wellness" in a twenty-item questionnaire in a pre- and double posttest. It verified that the experience contributed to significant gains on the Spiritual Well-Being Scale. Venable's research-based experimental curriculum focused on the trailcamping experience as a rites-of-passage ritual process with initiation as the peak celebration. Venable used journals kept by the campers, and a twenty-question spiritual well-being scale that was given before the camp, and then at four and twelve weeks after it. Though average scores rose across the board at the four-week mark, the scores of those who were guided through the ritual process by a mentor or other significant adult rose by more than five times over those who were accompanied by a parent. Even so, average scores on the religious well-being subscale rose for all campers at four and twelve weeks.

Over the years Christian camps have built toward a culminating worship service that calls on the campers to accept God's salvation and God's career call. *Christian Camping and Conference 1996/97 Survey Report* documents that more than 215,000 women and men are currently in career Christian ministry as a result of commitments they made at camp. Christian Camping International is an organization whose membership is composed primarily of denominationally affiliated and other religiously oriented camps and camping staff who design primarily traditional weeklong age-group, fixed-site camp programs.

Six dynamic principles are involved in the experience of religious camping. These principles give the camp experience its life and depth. *First, we are uprooted from our normal, everyday lives.* The experience of religious camping takes place outside the routine of our lives. It is something different—a special time apart.

Jesus' first command to his followers, "Follow me," implicitly required them to leave their old lives and livelihoods behind as they found new lives and identities with him. The transformation that occurred in each of them went beyond their established patterns of work, family, and relationships. They were called out of these patterns, not to make minor improvements in them but to find an entirely new way of living. Life as usual was totally disrupted as Jesus reshaped his followers. By allowing themselves to be uprooted, they also gained dependence on Jesus as he directed their re-formation.

Bob Cagle reminds us that in leaving home for camp we once again become a pilgrim people, a community of believers joined together as much by what we have left behind as where we are going. Worshiping in buildings of brick and wood, we forget that the early Israelites, our spiritual forebears, were tent-dwelling nomads who wandered from place to place, uprooted from place to be more firmly rooted in God. Religious camping is a time to uproot ourselves from ourselves and prepare to meet God.

Second, we are re-rooted in a place where we can grow in grace and faith. Having left our familiar lives behind, we find a new and fresh place we can once again call home. Being re-rooted refers to the camper's developing awareness that camp is a good place, a safe place. At the end of many five-day residential camps, a majority of campers express a desire for another week of camp. This is an indication that they have been re-rooted. In a sense, campers cannot find their real selves until they are re-rooted. Only after campers have left behind routine, family, friends, meals, music, and home are they able to see beyond these things to find themselves—or perhaps to be found by a watchful counselor or director.

It is in the process of re-rooting that re-creation can begin to take hold. In the new-found community and belongingness that being re-rooted in a camp setting provides, campers can make decisions concerning their future—decisions about religious commitments, jobs, lifestyles, friends, and callings.

The present authors have led backpacking trips that included a rite of passage. The teenage campers were given the opportunity to make a commitment to become the adults God created them to be. These initiations took place near the end of each trip, after each participant had an opportunity to re-root in their newly formed trail-family community. From this re-rooted vantage point, all teen campers pledged themselves to a new life in the future in which they would assume full responsibility for who they were becoming and for what they did.

Third, we experience the value and transforming power of relationships. It is difficult to describe what happens in the lives of campers, counselors, and directors alike as they enter into the experience of religious camping. When organized camping began decentralizing, that is, organizing around small groups of eight to twelve campers and a couple of counselors, it was not simply to remedy homesickness. Lois Goodrich identifies several advantages of the small group camp in her classic *Decentralized Camping*:

- promotes a quicker initial adjustment by the camper to the camping environment, helped by quickly learning the names of all small group members;
- allows the counselor to know and understand each individual camper better;
- intensifies personal relationships, allowing greater growth in shorter time;
- places greater responsibility on each small group member for the welfare of the entire group;
- highlights the reality of each member's importance to the group;
- provides a living situation in which campers can learn to face reality but cannot escape responsibilities, or avoid the dependence, love, and appreciation of other group members;
- provides a common base of understanding between campers that is not based on hometown, race, or nationality; and
- offers the best opportunity for taking home new skills acquired through small group living and interaction—skills that transfer to family life.

To the extent that strong and meaningful personal relationships are developed, campers are able to experience the incarnational reality of God among them. To be listened to, to be known, and to be affirmed— this is the heart of the transforming power of religious camping.

Fourth, ultimate respect for each camper as a unique creation and a living representation of God's love must always be shown. Whatever the goal of a particular religious camping program, such as evangelism or discipleship or experiencing God through nature, none of these can be accomplished until the basic needs of the campers have been met on an individual basis. This type of ultimate respect acknowledges that all campers bring to camp their own set of histories, needs, personalities, preferences, and life experiences. Bob Cagle asserts that a camper's personal history takes on a sacred dimension at camp. It is not the responsibility of counselors or directors to discard the objectives of the camp for the preferences of individual campers. But it is their responsibility to see that the basic needs of each camper—physical, emotional, and spiritual—are met, insofar as possible, in an authentic and personal way.

To maintain this high level of respect for the campers communicates the reality of each person's uniqueness and giftedness. Such respect conveys to all that they are valued and loved for who they are, just as they are, especially those who may feel either unloved or of little value.

As a rule, it is best to bring campers into the decision-making process about parts of the camp program. Input from the campers can help guide certain parts of the camp experience, and it distributes responsibility for the decisions made to everyone involved. Thus each camper is participating at a deeper level, not simply being present at camp, and is a willing participant in the overall experience.

Fifth, campers are initiated into a new way of living. Organized religious camping offers campers the opportunity to "try on" various elements of the adult world, along with the strength of an affirming community that celebrates differences and tolerates mistakes.

Camp can and should offer each camper freedom: freedom to learn new skills, freedom to fail and not be ridiculed, freedom to be oneself and be accepted by others, freedom to build self-esteem and trust in self and others.

Camping offers many youth a unique opportunity to be away from their parents' protection and rules. With this freedom comes responsibility. Whether it is in group-building activities, boating skills, challenge courses, or lunchroom courtesy, campers who shoulder new responsibilities should be recognized as adults in the making.

Sixth, campers live out the reality of the incarnation. In authentic religious camping, all involved are immersed in a close-knit community that reflects the reality of Jesus living and moving among us. Insofar as directors, counselors, and campers take the responsibility of developing meaningful relationships and genuinely showing ultimate respect for one another, the way will be paved for Jesus to live among us and to inhabit each person.

The saying "I'd rather see a sermon than hear one" is certainly true at camp, where there is no tolerance for mere display or empty words. As campers obey Jesus in their daily living, they move past knowing *about* Jesus to knowing *Jesus himself.*

THE POWER OF COMMUNITY

The glue that holds religious camping together, that explains why it changes lives and promotes meaningful discipleship, is the power of community. The transforming power of community offers life-changing hope to campers and staff alike.

The New Testament defines one of the Holy Spirit's tasks as the development of *koinonia,* or community, among believers. Research and experience have shown that small groups facilitate the growth of *koinonia.* Church growth author Howard Snyder writes that, in the mission of the gospel, church buildings may be superfluous, but small groups are not.

As campers are uprooted from their normal, everyday surroundings and are put together in small groups at camp, ordinary props are gone and campers have fewer masks to hide behind. But since everyone is in the same boat—temporarily rootless—a new common ground has already been established. The re-rooting that takes place bonds everyone through the power of community.

The power of community takes on an added dimension in the lives of Christians. Many religions believe that their gods inhabit a certain temple or town or prophet. But the Christian temple is a portable one, found in the risen Christ of the community. When we camp together, we do not find God in the chapel only or even in the beauty of nature surrounding the campground. God inhabits the sacred ritual space created by a small group of people, who seek the kingdom together and find Christ, arms open wide.

MORE RESOURCES TO HELP YOU FOLLOW UP WHAT YOU HAVE LEARNED FROM THIS CHAPTER

Cagle, Bob. *Youth Ministry Camping: A Start-to-Finish Guide to Helping Teenagers Experience the Greatness of God's Creation.* Loveland, Colo.: Group, 1989.
This is one of the most helpful books overall in the area of developing a ministry through camping.

Eells, Eleanor. *History of Organized Camping: The First 100 Years.* Martinsville, Ind.: American Camping Association, 1986.
Eells writes from the perspective of having lived through seventy of the first hundred years of camping.

Goodrich, Lois. *Decentralized Camping.* Updated ed. Martinsville, Ind.: American Camping Association, 1982.
This is a thorough, all-around aid to developing small group camping.

Snyder, Howard. *The Problem of Wineskins: Church Structure in a Technological Age.* Downers Grove, Ill.: InterVarsity, 1975.
A thoughtful discussion on using small groups effectively in local churches.

Venable, Stephen F. "Mountain Cathedrals: An Exploratory Study of Spiritual Growth of Teen-agers Through Backpacking." D.Min. diss., Asbury Theological Seminary, 1995.
An examination of teens' spiritual growth using one pre- and two posttests as well as guided journals during a five-day rite of passage-based backpacking experience.

3

SMALL GROUPS

In the intriguing—and horrifying—mid-1980s movie *The Breakfast Club,* five suburban high school students serve a Saturday detention together in the school library. It is important to note that when people find themselves in isolation, even as "prisoners," community happens. Before that fateful morning when the five students showed up for their punishment, only two of them knew each other by name. But they all knew each other as school stereotype labels: a brain, a jock, a beauty queen, a criminal, and a nerd. As the movie evolves and the plot plays out, the common humanity and pain shared by these five students, forgotten by their parents and ignored by the school, transforms them spirit and soul. They transcend their labels to become people with real names and real feelings, who connect at a deep level for the first time in their lives. A similar magic of community that occurs under duress is depicted in such movies as *White Squall* and *White Water Summer.* The power of a small group of humans undergoing shared experience is wonderful to behold.

THE DEVELOPMENT OF SMALL GROUPS AT CAMP

Some early camps were little more than schools with beds moved outdoors. Life was regulated and schedules were maintained, with everyone participating in all activities together. Often campers and staff hardly got to know each other. Sometime in the middle of the camping season of 1926, L. B. Sharp, then executive director of Life Camp, tossed out the old status quo and ushered in a new era in organized camping. Sharp decentralized camp.

The decentralized program, which evolved out of the Life Camp experience, refused to simply re-create activities and programs available in cities or other noncamp environments. The Life Camp took all that was special and unique about organized camping and transposed it into a higher key through the magic of small groups.

Camps were organized around small "family" groups with two counselors per group. Each small group was responsible for its own well-being, participation in the camp program, and welfare, insofar as possible. Camps differ as to how much autonomy they give small groups, but their success has made them an almost universal reality at virtually every camp across the country.

THE POWER OF SMALL GROUPS

E. Stanley Jones founded the Christian Ashram movement in 1930 while a missionary in India. What started out as "a vacation with God" developed into the practice of community with God through the fellowship of other Christians. In his book, *A Song of Ascents,* he rightly reflects that it was *koinonia* (community), not the church, that was born at Pentecost. That *koinonia* (the church is not mentioned until Acts 8) became the soul out of which the body, the church, would later grow. So where there is *koinonia*, there is the transforming power of God's Spirit. For Jones, this power was revealed in the company of other Christians camping together in communion with God.

The Lutheran pastor Dietrich Bonhoeffer belonged to a fellowship in an underground German seminary during the Nazi era. In his book *Life Together* Bonhoeffer combines practical advice and a theological discussion of the goals and hard work of Christian community. In Bonhoeffer's writings, Christian community and fellowship is not an ideal that *we* must work to realize. It is a reality that has been created by God in Christ in which we all may participate. Bonhoeffer stresses the need to recognize that ultimately all of our community is in Jesus Christ alone. There is no other basis for true fellowship.

As campers share their lives, they see and experience a reciprocal relationship. As they reveal themselves to one another, they also turn to one another for care, trust, and affirmation. These bonds are formed in the heat of self-disclosure and radical faith and are not easily broken.

SMALL GROUPS IN ACTION

Since the value of personal relationships is one of the central tenets of organized camping, even more so in religious camping where Jesus is present in every relationship through his incarnation, small groups should be structured and utilized in a way that facilitates and nurtures this invaluable resource.

The Servant/Leader Is Critical

Lois Goodrich says in *Decentralized Camping* that having the counselors living with the campers is *the* most important single element in the growth potential provided at camp. They eat, sleep, pray, worship, talk, share, laugh, cry, run, play, swim, maybe even get sick together. Indeed, camps provide opportunities for growth not only for campers but for the counselors as well. Some even say that counselors, who go to camp to serve the campers, have an even greater opportunity for growth. The lived-out willingness of the small group leaders to identify in every way and in every activity with their groups, creates the cohesion and transforming power of the group.

Diversity Is Required

Each small group should avoid including campers who already know each other. As a general rule of thumb, it is educationally sound to put no more than three friends or acquaintances together in a twelve-person group (fewer if the groups are smaller). This may not be possible at a very small camp, but the rule should be followed at every opportunity. Bringing together a small number of relative strangers allows all group members to immerse themselves in the camping experience slowly and with greater personal attention. Most important, all campers re-root with new roles, status, and high value.

In some camps, such as family and inter-generational camps, there is a wide diversity among campers. But breaking down camps and/or small groups by age or grade level is widely practiced.

Every Member Is Important

When a group assembles for the first time at camp, the counselor will probably notice a God-given diversity. Male/female, quiet/outgoing, attractive/plain, rowdy/reflective—*each member of every small group is important.* Valuing each member for who he or she is affords all campers the space and grace to reveal the image of God within them.

Building a Small Group Is an Ongoing Process

Since small groups are made of (sometimes frustratingly) different types of people, building that crew into a cohesive body is better seen as a process rather than as an instant accomplishment. From learning each other's names to building trust and sharing personal histories and dreams, growing a small group takes time and patience. The advantage of the camp environment is that it allows groups to spend virtually every daylight hour together in various activities designed to maximize the group-building and sharing process.

Denny Rydberg outlines five phases of group development in his book *Building Community in Youth Groups.* Briefly, these five phases are

- bond building: establishing trust,
- opening up: developing the freedom to hear and to be heard,
- affirmation: moving from *me* to *you* in a way that lifts up group members,
- stretching: learning vulnerability and acceptance through tough times, and
- deeper goal sharing and goal setting: developing accountability.

Each different phase requires activities and experiences in order to move through all five phases during a five-day camp, or even with an ongoing church youth group or Sunday school class. Learn to move slowly and discern when it's time to push to the next level.

Jesus Is Central

True *koinonia* (community) developed through relationships established in small groups is not the product simply of good and patient leadership or willing and open campers. Jesus is the central figure in each small group. Growing community is the ministry of Jesus. Camp directors and leaders simply plan and program effectively. The transforming power of *koinonia* is facilitated by small groups settings, but it is created by a visitation of Christ.

IMPLEMENTING SMALL-GROUP BASED CAMPING

The following suggestions deal with the specifics of setting up your camp in small groups that will facilitate growth and grace. *First, keep the small groups small.* Goodrich suggests about eight campers to a group. Although some camps may have more or fewer members, it is a good rule of thumb to keep the total group size at twelve or fewer. Jesus' own camping group of twelve disciples suggests that counselors can only invest in a few people if they are going to do it fully and bravely, with their whole lives.

Second, recruit open, caring leaders. The small group leaders have more to do with the groups' unity than the curriculum or the theme of the camp program. The group leaders should lead the way in openness, vulnerability, and concern for each small group member.

Third, plan for an adequate and varied small group time. In the sixth- and seventh- grade camp that Steve has codirected for more than a decade, small groups meet together intentionally for an hour in the morning and an hour in the evening. However, the groups also work together during camp cleanup, and they swim and hike together during recreation time. They play together during Bible games, work together at various crafts, and participate together in singing and drama events. They sit together at morning devotions, Bible study and evening worship. That is a lot of time together. Each activity is designed to build community within each small group.

Fourth, participate in the life of the camp. It is easy to get caught up in the needs of an individual small group, while neglecting the overall programming and thrust of the camp. Small groups should be afforded as much freedom and autonomy as possible, but they should participate fully in campwide activities as well.

If a small group begins to open up and share special concerns and problems just as worship is scheduled to begin, there is a dilemma of schedule versus spontaneity. While it is important to encourage sharing and to rejoice when a group begins to "click," the needs of the small group must be balanced with the overall design and goals of the camp as a whole. Thus the counselors should find a way to "report in" with camp directors about what is happening with their group and when it can be expected to make it to the next activity.

GROUP-BUILDING IDEAS

Counselors can pick from the following suggestions the ones that serve the goal and theme of the camp they are planning. Or they can be creative and develop their own small group activities.

Stand Up
Pair off in partners and sit on the ground with backs together, feet in front of you, and arms linked at the elbows behind you. Then try to stand up *together*. After a pair has succeeded, add another pair and try again. Keep adding people until your whole group is trying to stand together.

Jump
This is jumprope group style. Have the entire group form a circle, arms over shoulders. On the word **GO!**, everyone tries to jump with both feet off the ground, all at the same time. Once you have mastered this, try jumping with an imaginary rope with one person shouting out a cadence that gets progressively faster.

Copy Cat
Ask two volunteers to leave the group while you explain this game. One person is the leader. She casually does little things like scratching

her nose, crossing her legs, adjusting her glasses, and so on. The rest of the group copies her as subtly as possible. Choose someone to bring the two volunteers back to the group. Explain the activity without identifying the leader—they have to watch carefully and try to figure that out for themselves!

Candle with Care

Form a circle and have one member hold a lighted candle. The person with the candle begins by telling the group what he or she appreciates about one of the group members, without saying who is being talked about. The candle is passed to the person who was described. That person then describes another person and hands the candle off again. This should continue until everyone has been affirmed twice. The leader may need to watch that no one is neglected. (This exercise may also be done without candles if necessary.)

In the News

Each group member "interviews" another member (a stranger) for a fictitious camp newspaper. Give each group member a pencil and a handout that is prepared along the following guidelines:

1. Put a box in the upper right-hand corner with these instructions: Draw a picture of the person you're interviewing in the box. (Black and white only, please.)

2. Interview directions: Congratulations! You have been selected from hundreds of contestants to receive the Camper of the Week Award! We need the following information to include in the next edition of *Camp Chronicles*. What grade will you be in? What is your favorite subject in school? What do you think is the most boring subject in school? What extracurricular activities do you participate in? What is your favorite summer activity? What adult do you admire a lot? What is your favorite song? If you grew up to be famous, what kind of famous person would you

like to be (president, rock singer, movie star, inventor, clergy member, etc.)?

3. Add other questions that are consistent with the camp theme.

Who Am I
Prepare name tags with different Bible, cartoon or sports (or whatever) figures. Make each tag different. Gather the group in a circle and then walk around the outside of the circle, sticking a tag on each person's back. Then people mingle and ask each other yes or no questions about their identity. Members who have correctly guessed their identity can sit down.

Family Strength Quiz
Have each small group member answer these questions with yes, no or sometimes.

1. Are you nice to come home to?
2. When you are away, does the rest of the family look forward to your return?
3. Do you seek to "build up" your family?
4. Do you volunteer to help with any chores?
5. Are you proud of your parents?
6. Do you feel that your parents are proud of you?
7. Do you consistently obey your parents?
8. Do your parents listen to your point of view?
9. When you have a hassle with your family, do you seek to be helpful and forgiving?

Half Truth
One group member tells two things about himself or herself. One is true, the other is a lie. The group votes on which statement is true. The goal is to fool as many of the group members as possible.

Shy Charades

Each member of the group tells the whole group a personal fact such as place of birth, favorite hobby, favorite food, most dreaded vacation spot, career goal, and so on. The catch is that the information must be acted out, not spoken. Each member can announce the category (for example, favorite musical group), but the rest is to be communicated through gestures only.

Want Ad

Share the following information about yourself with the group to get some direction on what kind of career you might choose or on the direction God might be leading in your life:

- five things I am good at
- five things that I enjoy
- three jobs I have enjoyed
- three issues or causes that concern me
- one dream that keeps recurring.

Ropes or Challenge Course

If your campground has a ropes course or a challenge course, you can use it to build confidence and self-esteem in all group members. Begin with a safety discussion, perhaps with input from the course manager. Remind your group that the purpose of this activity is not to identify the most athletic member, but to build community within your group. After all the group members have looked over the course, ask them to share what part of it looks most difficult. Pray for one another. Use the following questions for discussion after everyone completes the course.

- Which part of the course was most difficult for you? What were you feeling as you experienced it?
- What were you thinking of as you completed the course?
- How did others' encouragement help you?

- How did it feel to be in a situation where you had to show weakness or apprehension in front of a group?
- What did you learn about trust and faith?
- How can you apply what you've learned to your relationships with others? With God?

MORE RESOURCES TO HELP YOU FOLLOW UP WHAT YOU HAVE LEARNED FROM THIS CHAPTER

Bannerman, Glenn, and Robert Fakkema. *Guide for Recreation Leaders.* Atlanta: Knox, 1975.
Guidelines and suggestions for group activities.

Bonhoeffer, Dietrich. *Life Together.* New York: Harper & Row, 1954.
An excellent discourse on Christian fellowship that arose out of the author's experience in an underground seminary in Germany during the Nazi years.

Coleman, Lyman. *Serendipity Youth Encyclopedia.* Littleton, Colo.: Serendipity House, 1985.
Chock-full of ideas for building small groups and holding interesting Bible studies.

Jones, E. Stanley. *Song of Ascents.* Nashville: Abingdon, 1968.
This autobiography of a world-witness Christian leader includes "The Ashram Note in My Song." The integrity of community based on the value of persons sets it apart from traditional ministries and organizations based on "power" and a "chain of command."

Rydberg, Denny. *Building Community in Youth Groups: Practical Models for Transforming Your Group into a Close, Caring Family.* Loveland, Colo.: Group, 1985.
Exercises designed to take groups through five phases of community development: bond building, opening up, affirmation, stretching, deeper sharing/goal setting.

4

CAMP BIBLE STUDY

The small group communities that are formed at camp create space in which deep human hungers can emerge. The camp environment is insulated from the rest of society, freeing campers of all ages to explore issues related to role, status, authority, and value. These have been driving forces in all cultures from prehistoric times. Tribal and survival communities all created ritual space in which to "make sense" of issues and experiences that threatened their lives or reduced them to captivity and abuse.

Camp community building tends to awaken these universal hungers and needs. There are appropriate ways to focus on the ageless wisdom and truth of the Judeo-Christian Scriptures when these deep hungers are awakened by the environment and the nature of the survival community in the camp setting. You can expect your campers to experience transforming growth through Bible study. This transformation does not occur in a vacuum or as a result of purely cognitive challenges. However, when the seeds of true community have been planted, they can be powerfully watered with the life-giving power of God's Word.

WHY STUDY THE BIBLE AT CAMP?

Camp participants can cultivate the perpetual human quest for God. They can identify with Moses going to the desert to worship; with Abraham seeking a place to call home; with Hannah desperately trying to understand why the family she wants is being denied her; with Nehemiah going home to rebuild the broken walls and restore what vandals have destroyed of his people's sacred home; with Mary responding in fear *and* obedience to surrender her life to God; with John the seer catching a glimpse of the heavenly kingdom. The very fabric of the campers' lives is woven throughout the pages of Scripture, if they only have eyes to see. Their search for God is age-old. The Bible contains an account of that search as well as of the Creator's quest for the created.

Persons who come to camp to find God face precisely that possibility, as well as the possibility of being found. Campers embark on the neverending challenge to grow in his grace, as they "all reflect the Lord's glory, [and] are being transformed into his likeness with ever-increasing glory, which comes from the Lord, who is the Spirit" (2 Cor 3:18 NIV).

The power of the small group community enables us to open up our lives to the mirror of Scripture. Then Scripture acts as the voice of God, calling campers to love and grace and discipleship through faith. When the formative impact of God's Word is removed from the camp community, God's call to radical life change does not ring out. Rather, corporate executives engage in team building.

Campers intentionally study the Bible at camp, not because that is what their parents did when they went to camp but because Bible study, like camp's natural setting, is a privileged avenue by which everyone experiences God.

PLANNING CAMP BIBLE STUDIES

There are two different approaches to preparing Bible studies. Each can be incorporated into the process of planning small group Bible studies for a camp setting.

Focus on Camper Needs

Bible story and principle need to be focused on deep issues of universal need and worry in order to make the most of the opportunity for life change that is created through the community of camp small groups. Since any group of campers represents very different learning styles, Bible teaching techniques should have a multiple target for styles and should pull together all perspectives in the community in the process of looking at ancient classical events or distillations of wisdom. So the counselor adapts to meet the camper and does not require the camper to change to meet the counselor's demand for point of view or "lesson."

Educator Bernice McCarthy has synthesized the learning style theory of David Kolb, the personality types writings of Carl Jung, the cognitive development studies of Jean Piaget, and recent research in left and right brain function differentiation to offer us a scheme for meeting all learners and synthesizing learning experiences. She calls her teaching plan *the 4-MAT system.* She identifies four basic learning styles or preferences:

- imaginative learners who prefer to sense, feel, and watch
- analytic learners who prefer to think and watch
- common sense learners who like to think and do
- dynamic learners who like to sense, feel, and do

When leading a small group Bible study, the counselor addresses each learning style by moving from concrete experience to reflection

Figure 4.1
The Learning Process

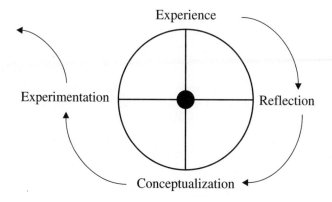

Figure 4.2
Teaching Activities for the Four Learning Styles

Contrete Experience (What?)	Reflective Observation (Why?)	Abstract Conceptualization (How?)	Active Experimentation (Do it!)
Case story	Solve problems.	Summarize principles.	Apply to a personal challenge.
Reenacted story skit	Define questions which expose issues.	Analyze: how to avoid repeating and to solve.	Write a memo to self: Never forget this!
Video or story song	Brainstorm— What bothered you?	Prioritize, rank order and resolve problems.	Report to group what you need to do as a result.
Parable	Translate to present.	Summarize meanings.	Act on new wisdom.

to conceptualization and then launching campers into experimentation to act on what was taught, thus meeting the learning needs of each of them. Picture the process as a wheel. First, you re-create an experience, then you guide reflection on a case, parable, or story, then you move on to develop a wisdom or theoretical base and help the learners own the concept(s) being explored, and finally learners integrate their learning into personal decisions and actions.

In the first quadrant the leader re-creates an experience, in the second quadrant the group reflects on that experience, in the third quadrant the leader teaches the concept(s), and in the fourth quadrant the leader steps back and allows the campers to teach themselves and others by living it out.

Following is a sample Bible study lesson that uses the 4-MAT system. This lesson on family (Lk 15:11–32) is taken from a high school camp curriculum written by Steve.

I. Act it out (concrete story)

Have the small group act out the story of the prodigal son (Lk 15:11–32), making up their own modern characters. For instance, have the father be the owner of an all-night muffler shop and have the younger son work at a video arcade cleaning the rest rooms for game tokens after he runs out of money. Be creative! Have the campers act out the story. Let the group member playing the younger son say what he thinks that son should say to his father. Afterward, ask those playing the father and older son what their response would be to the younger son's return. (An alternative to acting out the story is viewing the ten-minute music video *A Father and Two Sons*, produced by the American Bible Society.)

II. Find it out (reflection)

Now read or paraphrase or have a small group member read Luke 15:11–32. Ask these questions:

- Who in the story do you most want to be like, and why?
- Why did the lost son's father consider the lost son important?
- Describe a time when you felt as loved and accepted as the lost son felt when he returned to his dad.
- Describe a time when you wish you had felt so loved and accepted.
- Find ways in which the "lost" son and the son who stayed home can work out their shared pain.

III. What does it mean? (conceptualization)

Note the following:

- It is generally understood that in Jesus' day asking for your inheritance while your father was still living was the equivalent of saying, "I wish you were dead!"
- Based on Old Testament law, younger sons got less inheritance than the eldest son.

- The father's love for his sons extends beyond the disobedience and rejection they showed him.
- Though the younger son returned home hoping for a place as a slave, he was accepted back as a son.
- In Jesus' culture eating a meal with an enemy symbolized forgiveness and reconciliation. The father's elaborate celebration for his son represents the extent of his great love.
- God loves and accepts us just as deeply as the father who took back his son.

IV. What are you going to do about it? (experimentation)

Ask how we can best respond to God's tremendous love for us. After some members have responded, hand out copies of the following personal response sheet (using the questions below) and pencils. The sheets can be filled out either by writing out the answers to the questions or by drawing a picture of you "coming home" to God, as the younger son came home to his father. A camper who has not experienced "coming home" can conjecture how such a homecoming might look and feel like.

Two Kinds of Knowing

Thomas Groome's shared praxis model of religious education seeks to link what we know and learn with who we are. Here the small group members' personal stories are brought together with the Christian story to allow them to move beyond simply knowing about God to possessing an intimate, owned knowledge of God, a place where they can make informed decisions about how they choose to live out their faith. This model highlights our need to know God personally through experience, relationship, and response.

Groome calls his approach "experience/story/vision." It attempts to bring together each participant's personal stories and experiences (expressed with a lower case s and v) with the sacred Story/Vision (always capitalized) of the whole faith tradition of the Christian people and Scripture. The Christian vision includes our lived response that the story invites us in to, as well as the promises God makes to us

Figure 4.3
Personal Response Sheet

What Are You Going to Do about It?

Either answer the questions below or draw a picture on the back that symbolizes your "coming home" to God, as the younger son came home to his father.

1. If I am going to live like God's beloved child, then I am going to have to do the following things (list at least three on back):
2. To maintain proper relationships with my parents and family, I choose to do the following (list at least three on back):
3. I want to obey Jesus, but I am not always sure. Here are some questions I still have (list them on back):

Today I am making a promise to live out a positive response to God's deep love for me, symbolized by the father's love for his children in Luke 15:11–32. I will try to follow him and seek his help in my family relationships, no matter how hard it may seem.

Signed:
Dated:

---

from within the story. The following six steps summarize the E/S/V process.

1. Focusing activity. This step is similar to the *4-MAT* concrete story step. Participants' "stories" are the magic that calls everyone into primal issues and reflection. Or you can build around a song, perform a skit, watch a video, or use some other concrete activity to focus the campers' attention on what is being taught.
2. Naming our knowing. This step brings campers to an awareness to what they already know based on their experience and life circumstances.
3. Reflection on our knowing. Here campers are invited to share their own personal life stories and relate them to the specific concerns of the day's lesson.

4. The Christian community Story and Vision. Here is where the campers discover the broader knowledge that comes from the community of faith—from Holy Scripture. Here everyone begins to grapple with the personal faith response it invokes.
5. Dialogue between the Story and the campers' stories. Now participants see that the way they live out their faith must be informed by the biblical message as this message is taken and owned personally by them.
6. Dialogue between Vision and participants' vision. At this point each participant is empowered to willingly choose a faith response in light of all that has gone on before.

Groome's model has two strengths as a method for camp Bible studies. First, the Christian Story/Vision is presented in an open-ended manner, one that invites active dialogue with the Story/Vision rather than passive reception of the Bible study leader's teaching. The counselor works toward *disclosure* rather than *closure* so the discussion responses stirred within the campers can grow until the response it demands is met honestly and thoroughly. Second, this method takes seriously the Christian truth that knowing God is more than simply knowing about God. Each camper and each leader must be given the opportunity to know God and to live out that knowledge through a changed life.

The following Bible study, Where Am I Going? (1 Cor 13:11–12), attempts to illustrate Groome's E/S/V model. Steve wrote it for middle school campers.

I. Focusing activity

Have each camper act out, without words, actions associated with growing up or childhood while the other campers guess what they're doing.

II. Naming our knowing

Let the campers share changes they have gone through already in life that have brought them to where they are now.

III. Reflecting on our knowing
Ask each camper to share a special personal story: "The best thing that ever happened to me was when . . ."

IV. The Christian community Story and Vision
Have a camper read 1 Corinthians 13:11–12.

V. Dialogue between the Scripture Story and campers' stories
Ask, "What are some of the ways that camp and our small group are helping you grow up and become an adult? What do you see inside yourself when you look at the mirror of your life? What is God wanting to see?"

VI. Dialogue between Vision and participants' vision
In smaller groups of two or three, ask the campers to share what they need to change in their lives in order to put childish ways behind them. Then have them pray for one another asking for strength to follow God.

LEADING A SMALL GROUP BIBLE STUDY

The following suggestions offer tips for leading a motivating and transforming study of the Bible in a small group.

1. The group leader needs to operate like a compass, that points the way, rather than an encyclopedia, that has all the answers. The leader should function as an assuring guide, a companion on a journey, not a know-it-all teacher who has already arrived.

2. Every member of the group (including the leader) should be prepared to grow and learn and respond to the Scripture message. We lead by example.

3 Ask open-ended questions that make participants think and explore their feelings rather than closed-ended questions that only need a simple yes, no, I guess so, or yeah.

4. Try to get everyone engaged in the process early in the meeting. It is difficult to involve someone who checks out during the first fifteen minutes of a session.

5. Do not be afraid of silence. Leaders should give everyone time to think through what is going on and should not be too quick to bail themselves or someone else out of a dilemma.

6. Mix things up, using a variety of teaching styles and techniques, to interest everyone at various levels.

PUTTING IT ALL TOGETHER

Now that we have looked at the power of small groups and at planning and leading small group Bible studies, it is time to pull it all together into a unified camp curriculum package. Give a copy of the camp curriculum to each small group leader as a guide to the camp's purpose, theme, goals, procedures, schedule, and activities. Here is a list of handy items to include in the curriculum:

1. Camp title, theme, logo, song, goals, and brief statement of purpose

2. Daily guides for small group meetings, including a list of teaching objectives and supplies needed for each meeting, as well as an outline of the Bible study or other small group search for significance, power, and meaning planned for that meeting. Small group meeting times can begin with group-building activities, and then move into Bible study/response time. The activities should promote increasing personal vulnerability and risk taking as the week progresses and community begins to form.

3. Reminders for preparations or special needs for the following small group session included at the end of each meeting

4. A single copy of each handout to be used included in the curriculum

5. Daily schedule with times and places for each activity

6. Schedules for special activities that are done in small groups, like cleaning, setting tables, and engaging in crafts, broken down by day and time, listing the names of small groups participating

MORE RESOURCES TO HELP YOU FOLLOW UP WHAT YOU HAVE LEARNED FROM THIS CHAPTER

Coleman, Lyman, et. al., eds. *The NIV Serendipity Bible for Study Groups.* Grand Rapids: Zondervan, 1988.
A great resource full of open/dig/reflect questions and observations as well as pages of reproducible worksheets.

Groome, Thomas H. *Christian Education: Sharing Our Story and Vision.* New York: Harper & Row, 1980.
Groome's experience/story/vision procedure for religious education represents a breakthrough in moving from knowledge about God to knowledge of God, that is, knowing God.

McCarthy, Bernice. *The 4-MAT System: Teaching to Learning Styles with Right/Left Mode Techniques.* Rev. Ed. Barrington, Ill.: Excel, 1987.
The 4-MAT system allows teachers to teach to every learning style.

McNabb, Bill, and Steven Mabry. *Teaching the Bible Creatively: How to Awaken Your Kids to Scripture.* Grand Rapids, Mich.: Zondervan/Youth Specialties, 1990.
A moving and varied collection of over a dozen easy-to-read and apply principles for teaching the Bible, with over fifty program ideas you can start using *now*.

The Youth Worker's Encyclopedia of Bible-Teaching Ideas: Old Testament & New Testament. 2 vol. Loveland, Colo.: Group, 1994.
These two volumes include ideas for motivating scriptural principles from every book of the Bible, plus games, retreat plans, special projects, prayers, music, skits, and so on.

5

WORSHIP AT CAMP

"When I got on the bus at our church in Houston, I knew I was going to meet God this weekend." The speaker was about fourteen years old. One of the Communion servers brought him to me (Don) in tears during the Sunday morning communion service at Lakeview Camp.

After taking him into an alcove to listen to his story and to pray with him, I sent him back: "Now you are ready to take Holy Communion. You are God's new man."

The entire weekend at Lakeview had been orchestrated to draw teens toward the worship of God in a full service climaxing with Holy Communion. The singing, the response to Scripture, and the sermon calling for obedience to Jesus' call to "be holy, as your Father in heaven is holy" opened the door to personal worship, an invitation to kneel at the altar and to receive the cup and the bread—signs of betrothal to Jesus.

After all six hundred campers had been served at the altar, I described the fourteen-year-old's personal response. "If you are here today and you need to be on your knees once more right now to settle things with Jesus in making specific confession, in accepting Jesus' claims on you, or in seeking to know Jesus personally, let's open the altar once more just for personal prayer."

More than fifty campers responded immediately. The camp schedule for the noon meal had to wait while God came surprisingly near, just as God had promised the young man as he stepped on the bus in Houston.

- What brought the teenagers to this point of response?
- What do campers bring to the altar?
- What will they do with what they have seen and heard?
- How will their relationships with others be affected by their encounters with God at camp?

- What vision of God is being formed and molded during worship at camp?

WHAT IS WORSHIP?

Camp worship experiences are more than opportunities to stand in a pew, clap or raise hands, kneel to pray, or hold someone's hand during a prayer. Worship is more than this action or that one. Yet, paradoxically, it encompasses all humanity ever does at any given moment. No one is changed except in "ritual space." Worship consists of creating ritual space in which God comes near because the worship is directed toward God. Paul even wrote, "Therefore, I urge you, . . . in view of God's mercy, to offer your bodies as living sacrifices, holy and pleasing to God—this is your spiritual act of worship" (Rom 12:1 NIV, emphasis added).

Thus, worship involves:

- our response to God,
- receiving God's mercy,
- reordering our lives, and
- revealing God to others

Respond
The truth is that humans cannot respond to God unless he calls them. When people begin to ask spiritual questions, and to seek God, we can be sure God is already at work in their lives. Jesus said, "No one can come to me unless the Father who sent me draws him." (Jn 6:44a NIV).

In worship, human beings respond in worship to the relationship God offers to them. Through deliberately orchestrated acts people offer their lives to their Creator in praise and adoration. But God reached out to humanity first. Worship is not confined to what goes on in a church sanctuary on Sunday morning, nor even to an event at religious camps. Rather, worship—connection and response to God—is a defining mark of all who are acknowledging that human beings have received God's grace in their lives.

Receive

God has reached out to everyone, and many respond. Then they begin the lifelong process of receiving God into their lives in ever deeper ways. "Every good and perfect gift is from above, coming down from the Father of the heavenly lights" (Jas 1:17 NIV). People receive God at the reading of God's Word. They receive God through the singing of a song. They receive God through a message shared or a sermon preached. They receive God in the power of forgiveness and reconciliation. They receive God in breaking the bread and sharing the cup of Communion. Once persons respond to God's invitation to relationship, they open themselves up to receive God's presence.

Reorder

As persons encounter God through worship, they are reconciled to God and re-created in God's image, and their lives take on new character and new priorities. However, this reordering of their lives is not a list of resolutions about what persons plan to do for God. Rather it is a reflection of God's ongoing grace in their lives. This is the point of tremendous personal change as well as tremendous personal resistance. Many call this point of possible worship a crisis of belief. Do we truly believe God is God? Are we ready to follow God *wherever* God leads us? Have we counted the cost? Are we willing to pay the price of obedience? This encounter is a crisis because we cannot both stay where we are and go with God.

Reveal

Once persons respond to God's invitation to relationship, begin to receive God's works of grace and to reorder the foundational priorities in their lives, they are ready and prepared to reveal God to others. Paul wrote in II Corinthians 3:18, "And we, who with unveiled faces all reflect the Lord's glory, are being transformed into his likeness with ever-increasing glory, which comes from the Lord, who is the Spirit" (NIV). Revealing God to others involves both personal transformation and transparency. Here persons share with their words and their actions God's ongoing work in their lives. Sometimes persons share God consciously, at other times without even realizing it. When persons reveal God, they make him known through the witness of his work in their own lives.

TYPES OF CAMP WORSHIP SERVICES

The following suggestions show how the time, place, and style of worship can be varied at camp:

- Sunrise/sunset services. Find a scenic location at the campground you are using, where you can watch the beginning or ending of the day together. Use this time to reflect on the wonder of God's creation, new beginnings or endings, and so on.
- Special meals. Set a meal apart for a special observance of gratitude and thanks. This will involve more than offering a prayer of thanks. Convene a silent "monk's meal." The meal is shared in silence, all diners sit with campers they do not know and intentionally get to know each other. Then they thank God for new friends. Conclude the meal with having campers state what they are most thankful for at the camp.
- Evening worship. Many Christian camps close the day with a celebration worship service. Campers gather to sing and praise, to share the good things that have gone on at camp that day, and to offer themselves—even their very lives—back to God.
- Closing worship. A culminating worship service is a wonderful way to end a camp experience. This service returns the gifts offered and received at camp back to the Giver. This is a great opportunity to have campers share from their hearts how they have been touched and transformed during their time at camp.

PROGRAMMING FOR
MEANINGFUL WORSHIP AT CAMP

Responding to God in worship can be a life-changing experience for campers and for counselors as well. Thus it is important to be creative when planning camp worship, introducing variety in setting, mood, style, and method.

Singing

The Psalmist wrote (or sang):

> Give thanks to the Lord, call on his
> name;
>   make known among the nations
> what he has done.
> Sing to him, sing praise to him;
>   tell of all his wonderful acts (Ps 105:1–2 NIV).

Music and singing were incorporated into worship long ago. Today many churches sing both traditional hymns and contemporary praise choruses.

Campers like to sing a wide variety of music. You can sing a blessing before a meal, as the camp gathers for Bible study, before an announcement, during a nature hike, at a worship service, or while campers are gathered at an altar for prayer. Jim Marian describes six categories of songs that are appropriate for youth.

1. Upbeat songs: fun or crazy songs with limited spiritual significance
2. Celebration songs: faster songs celebrating the Christian life or describing God
3. Call to worship songs: songs encouraging the worshipers to focus on God and enter into God's presence (moderate tempo aids in transition)

4. Praise songs: songs extolling God, the Christian life, or the attributes of God (generally slower, quieter songs); speaking about God or directly to God

5. Introspective songs of petition to God: quiet, intense songs asking for God's help in our Christian walk

6. Intimate songs of worship: intense songs (usually having a slow or moderate tempo) directed exclusively to God

Camp leaders should dip deeply into the music resources of their tradition and use these six items as a checklist to enrich their music diet. One or more songs from each of these categories can be used to lead the campers away from the busyness and activities of the day into the presence of the living God. The progression here is geared toward a positive transition into life-changing worship.

Worship Leader

A good singer is not the same as a gifted worship leader, although both can be outstanding examples of Christian virtue and devotion. Both can enhance the quantity and quality of camp worship experiences. Both can have a calling to minister to and with the children of God. But when it comes to corporate camp worship, the singer performs and the leader facilitates.

The worship leader is the one to lead worship at camp, since leadership is much more important than polished skill or talent. One year Steve arranged for a performer (a former talent show winner, no less) to come to lead worship at the middle school camp he codirects. This proved to be a mistake. She was ready and able to perform morning, noon, and night. But the campers soon grew weary of hearing her, and wanted to do some singing themselves. The next year Steve's wife Cindy suggested asking Todd, an area youth director, to come and lead worship. He could play the guitar, but his singing voice was not broadcast quality and he had a reputation for hanging out with teenagers, not leading public worship. Somehow, however, Cindy's judgment seemed right. That summer and the two following summers,

Todd was the best worship leader we had had at the camp. When Todd left, his protege came and amazed everyone with his understanding of worship, and his ability to lead young people to worship.

As this story illustrates, a good worship leader

- lives a life of worship (connection with God),
- probably knows more about worship than about music theory,
- works better with people than with instruments or tape decks, and
- is much more interested in leading others into meaningful worship than displaying personal talents

Music

Newer music technologies offer rich options for music accompaniment at camp. These include split-track and accompaniment tapes and CDs, electronic keyboards, and other instruments. The standard acoustic guitar and piano are still important accompaniment resources as well and demonstrate the wide variety of options available. Before you decide what type of music resources to use, give some thought to the following considerations:

- What equipment is available? Who can operate it?
- The size of the camp. The number of worship leaders and musicians should be proportionate to the number of campers.
- How much music you plan to incorporate into worship.

Always bear in mind that the purpose of worship is to respond to God's invitation to relationship. Use musical instruments and equipment to lead the campers into worship. Avoid letting them be a hindrance or distraction.

Teaching for Worship and Praise

It is helpful to allot time for teaching campers the meaning and purpose of worship, and then giving them an opportunity to practice it. After Todd came to lead worship at the middle school camp, the leadership team decided to allot an hour for a worship seminar during the middle three days of the five-day camp. A third of the campers chose to study worship leadership. They sang and they learned about the meaning of Christian worship through teaching, example, and practice. These young teens worked together with the worship leader to prepare a new song, which they taught to all of us at corporate worship that evening. Since that experience we have used former campers who learned about and created the ritual space of worship at our camp to lead the next generation in praise and worship.

Preaching

Preaching at camp is an art. It is also a team activity that is most effective when it is unified by the theme, content, and direction of the camp as a whole and when the camp preacher is a full-time participant in the life and activities of the camp.

Here are some additional suggestions for enhancing the impact of the preaching at camp:

- Preachers serves as advocates for God to the campers and as the campers' advocate to God. Camp preachers of all kinds— prophets, exhorters, teachers—can come to the campers and encourage them from the standpoint of their own life struggles and concerns. The person preaching should never ridicule individual campers or draw negative attention to them.
- Target the campers where they are. Depending on the age of the campers, sermons should be brief, story based, and creative. This is not a time to pull one out of the Sunday morning church files. Sermons for elementary campers can be given in character. Dress and speak to the campers as Abraham, Moses, John, Paul, or a character from one of Jesus' parables.
- Preach to motivate and to encourage life change that the campers can take home with them. Address real-life issues that relate to the camp theme from a biblical perspective.
- Keep the focus on Jesus and the reality of his presence at home as well as at camp.

Drama and Worship

Incorporating appropriate drama into worship provides another window through which we can view the mystery of God at work in the lives of his children. The counselor can incorporate a drama seminar into the camp schedule and include campers in drama during worship. The following practical tips maximize the effectiveness of drama in camp worship.

- A drama teacher is like a worship leader—a facilitator, not just a performer.
- Make sure the dramas tie into the theme of the camp.
- Use various types of drama. Try acting out plays, biblical stories, mimes, verba-mimes (drama set to a song, similar to a live music video), and others.
- Involve as many of the campers as possible.

Ministry and Worship

When ten lepers were cured, one of them returned to Jesus and praised God (Lk 17:11–19). The others simply went on their way. Each person responds to camp worship experiences differently. Sometimes worshipers need the guidance of someone else who can reassure them, pray for them, and strengthen them in the decisions made and the experiences realized through worship. When campers respond to worship by way of expressing personal needs and reaching out for help, adults and/or older campers should be ready to encourage and aid them in interpreting the movement of God in their lives.

- The response of campers to worship should be considered seriously, individually, and confidentially. Give the campers time and space to express themselves and listen to what they say.
- During personal ministry times in response to worship, counselors should minister in public view of other worshipers or should recruit a friend of the young person to be present if the counselor needs to find private space for counsel and prayer.

Spiritual and sexual vulnerability tend to occur together, so integrity in counseling becomes critical as an act of fidelity to God.

Sharing and Testimonies

A critical but often overlooked need in camp worship is providing the campers with the opportunity to share how God has touched them and what they will take home with them from their experiences at camp. The camp program should allow time, either daily or at the end of camp, for campers to express what camp has meant to them. With guidance from the appropriate leaders, some campers may want to share a song, perform a drama, or read a Scripture. The counselors should give them as much latitude as possible to encourage and validate their responses.

OTHER WAYS WE WORSHIP AT CAMP

Since worship is a life response to God, it involves much more than a sunrise gathering or a preaching service at camp. After Pentecost, the early Christians "devoted themselves to the apostles' teaching and to the fellowship, to the breaking of bread and to prayer" (Acts 2:42 NIV).

Some other valuable activities that are not always seen as worship include:

- Bible studies that open up God's Word in new and compelling ways (see chap. 4),
- small group fellowship, formal and informal, in the cabins and between activities (counselors watching for what God is doing among the campers),
- sharing meals together (an eye-opening glimpse into the work that God is doing in the campers' lives; counselors should join campers in the dining hall and share Communion together as a camp in thanks for what God has done for all), and

- respect for the primacy of prayer as an act of worship, not just an obligation before a meal or an opportunity to put in a request (seek God through prayer, asking that God make himself known to yourself and the campers).

MORE RESOURCES TO HELP YOU FOLLOW UP WHAT YOU HAVE LEARNED FROM THIS CHAPTER

Cagle, Bob. *Youth Ministry Camping: A Start to Finish Guide to Helping Teenagers Experience the Greatness of God's Creation.* Loveland, Colo.: Group, 1989.
Chapter 13 has some good material, including ready-to-use ideas and outlines for creative camp worship.

Foster, Richard. *Celebration of Discipline: The Path to Spiritual Growth.* Revised Edition. New York: Harper & Row, 1988.
From this modern-day classic you will learn how to make worship a way of life.

Marian, Jim. *Leading Your Students in Worship: How to Plan and Lead Dynamic Singing to Help Students Grow Closer to God.* Wheaton, Ill.: Victor, 1993.
A practical and helpful guide to making worship and singing a priority in youth ministry.

Nappa, Mike, and Amy Nappa. *Bore No More: 70 Creative Ways to Involve Your Audience in Unforgettable Bible Teaching.* Loveland, Colo.: Group, 1995.
Great active and interactive illustrations and suggestions for involving others in memorable preaching or teaching.

Super Plays for Worship and Special Occasions. Loveland, Colo.: Group, 1994.
Several great plays, plus tons of hints and tips on directing, staging, and production.

6

CAMP COUNSELORS

A few years ago Steve codirected a high school backpacking trip in the Weminuche wilderness area of southwestern Colorado. The leadership team for this trip made two fatal errors: there were too many campers and too few counselors. It was one of the worst experiences of Steve's life. Things got off to a bad start as a camper was injured on the first day of the hike. The camper had to be airlifted to a local hospital, with one of the few counselors accompanying him. When it became clear that the backpacking trip had to be aborted, a group of angry campers had to trudge out of the wilderness and back home to Texas.

When the counselors decided to go back down the mountain, Steve wept spontaneously. Not because the trip had been planned so poorly or because his days in the beauty of God's creation were cut short. Not so much because a camper had been injured, since he trusted his recovery to God. He was weeping because circumstances had forced him to become more of a commandant than a friend or a counselor or a wise backpacker or a beloved mentor. He was forced to make a decision unilaterally. Instead of facilitating and demonstrating and participating and blessing, he was abrupt with people, correcting and rebuking and feeling isolated from counselors and parents as well as from teenage campers. Steve made a promise that if he ever led another backpacking trip (as he has done every year since), it would never leave home under the same conditions. The privilege of being with (instead of against) a staff of counselors and a group of teenage campers is too great a pleasure to damage or destroy for any reason.

WHAT IS A CAMP COUNSELOR?

Whatever the setting, whatever the purpose, whatever the goals, every camp needs counselors. Even an adult camp needs a program director or people facilitator. Camp counselors serve many different roles, depending on the occasion and the need, and include the following:

- *Spiritual compass and guide.* A camp counselor does not need to be a beatific saint, memorize half the Bible, or be a religious professional, such as a clergy member or seminarian. In the sense that life with God is a journey, the camp counselor should be committed to that pilgrimage and should be able to illuminate at least the part of the road, blessing the campers on their way.
- *Facilitator/empowerer.* In this role, counselors respond to particular camp activities and involve the campers. They draw the campers into the life and meaning of the camp through a wide variety of activities, and they find the areas in which each camper is most comfortable.
- *Responder.* Camp counselors respond to the needs of the campers, adapting teachable moments to the needs and dispositions of the campers in their charge. Whether it is time to pray, listen, talk, discuss, encourage, or whatever, counselors attempt to stay in tune with the needs of their groups.
- *Translator.* A translator is someone who acts as a bridge between the various camp experiences and the meaning of these experiences in the lives of the campers. A translator does not prescribe the meaning of any particular camp experience but helps campers to integrate experiences through interpreting their meaning for them, thus promoting growth.
- *Participant.* Camp counselors are also key players on the leadership team (see chap. 10). Counselors are active participants in sharing responsibilities at all levels of camp activities. It is as leader-participants that they truly serve as spiritual guides, facilitator/empowerers, responders, and translators. Counselors are responsible to the campers to join them at the very point of their involvement in the camp experience.

POTENTIAL CAMP COUNSELORS

There is no single profile for the ideal counselor. But there are some questions that program leaders can ask and groups can look to as they search for those who are willing and able to serve.

- Is the potential counselor willing to share his or her faith through personal example as well as through camp interactions (for example, small groups, sharing times, Bible studies, one-on-one caring and listening, and so forth)?
- Does the candidate work well with the age-group that the camp serves? Some counselors work better with high school campers, while others seem to understand and relate better to middle schoolers. Still others enjoy elementary school children. Find the counselors who match the needs of your camp.
- Does the candidate show an openness and vulnerability that will allow them to participate in camp experiences with the campers, while facilitating their learning and growth?
- Can the candidate focus on the campers? Some counselors come to camp hoping to find relief from their own personal pain and struggles. Counselors must be able to set aside personal goals and participate in a religious education ministry to campers. Counselors are almost always blessed and strengthened and encouraged. But they must come to camp ready to rally their personal strength and energy around the campers, not their own needs.

The world is full of potential camp counselors, although they may be more easily overlooked than found. We need to see with eyes that can identify potential and opportunity, eyes that see through the everyday world to the world of new possibilities found at camp. There are groups from which we intentionally draw camp counselors. It is important for camp leaders to be creative and purposeful, and use as many different types of counselors as possible. No perfect ratio exists to quantify the number of people to be drawn from each group. Achieving a proper balance is difficult but crucial.

Parents

These people have toiled along the road with their own children, and other young people have seen them at church. They have visited in their homes and have seen them "in action," admiring them from a distance. Although it is not appropriate to put campers' parents in the same cabin with them, camp is a fine opportunity for parents to put their skills and wisdom front and center, and reach out to other kids in a healthy motherly or fatherly way.

Grandparents

Depending on the rigors of the camp and on the health of the grandparents, their presence at camp can produce an inspiring intergenerational experience. Some will be able to do hiking or rock climbing, while others can be placed in the dining hall or craft areas. Scattered around the cabins or small groups, they draw campers with their love and wisdom. Be creative. If grandparents are willing and able to come to your camp, places should be found for them, even if this has never been done before.

Young Adults

Because of their relative personal freedom, many college-age young adults are ready and able to become role models for younger children at camp. These are people who can relate to the campers because they have just been where they are. They can understand their struggles and can show them in a very concrete way that there is life beyond where they are. Many young adults will be getting involved in hands-on religious education ministry for the first time. Some will serve as summer youth directors, while others will be involved in churches on a volunteer basis. Camp extends the opportunity to learn by doing and touch the lives of many campers in the process. Young adult counselors tend to be a little more energetic (read "wild") and less inhibited (read "crazy"), ready and able to help the younger campers spin off some of their excess energy.

Counselor Trainees

Every camp should maintain some sort of counselor training program, whether formal or informal. Steve's entire family attends our middle school camp each summer. With two young children, Steve and his wife started taking a teenage nanny to help with child care. It was not long before the nanny had graduated to full counselor status. At other times the family has taken camp helpers, who are just a few years older than our middle school campers, to run errands, coordinate an activity, or provide other support as needed. Before long, they can serve capably as full-blown counselors. It is wise to begin this year to prepare and train next year's counselors.

RESPONSIBILITIES OF CAMP COUNSELORS

Asking people to serve as camp counselors is asking for their lives, not just their skills and talents. Different counselors assume differing responsibilities, but they present themselves for ministry during the camp because they love the children, not because they can interpret nature or lead a Bible study or play the guitar. Leaders should not make the mistake of choosing "talented" counselors over "caring" counselors. Anyone who is unable to care should not be on the camp leadership team. Caring is an essential component in camping personnel.

- Camp counselors should live out the reality of a transformed and transforming life. Their witness to a life of growing obedience to Jesus should be transparent to all.
- They must eat, drink, and breathe campers, campers, campers during the camp. If the camp is based on a small group model, the counselors must be consumed with where their groups are physically, emotionally, and spiritually, and they should wrap their lives around the needs of the group and the goals and direction of the camp in general. This includes getting to know their campers on a personal level. Campers should be valued enough that their counselors call them by their first names.

- Counselors are responsible for the physical safety of the campers. They should monitor the safety of their campers in all activities, should be prepared to administer at least rudimentary first aid if necessary, and should stand prepared to get additional help as needed.
- Counselors also protect the emotional and spiritual health of the campers. They should discourage (never participate in) jokes or teasing based on race, ability, appearance, aptitude, or economic status. Joking must be at counselor expense, never at the expense of a camper.
- In the cabins counselors promote order and attempt to insure that everyone's personal space and property are respected. They monitor the camper's basic needs, such as rest or sleep. Counselors who have not successfully negotiated their own "adolescence" may be a menace to teen campers, who will be confused by a counselor who seems to be stuck in unending irresponsibility.
- Counselors must work with campers in the ways defined by the leadership team and by the clear goals of the camp. Whether they are needed to lead a small reflection group, lead a nature hike, join in a worship drama program, or give a cabin devotional, counselors should be flexible and prepared. The counselors' equipment and program needs are met by the leadership team.
- Though evangelism may be a primary issue for the camp leadership and/or counselors, it must follow, not prematurely precede, personal relationships between counselor and campers—a relationship in which the campers know they are safe and valued and loved as individuals.

TRAINING CAMP COUNSELORS

Training for camp counselors varies in different types of camps. Some camps use an overnight or a weekend time frame to develop counselor recruits into a shared mission leadership team. Other camps bring in their counselors for orientation a few hours before campers are scheduled to arrive. Still other camps will recruit only adults who possess the necessary skills for that camp experience. Such might include specialty camps for campers with physical or mental handicapping conditions. Another specialty camp might be a backpacking camp that requires experience in the wilderness or a winter camp that calls for experience in dealing with the cold.

Camp counselor training is an essential feature for every camp. Every camp is different, and every mix of leadership, counselors, and campers is unique. The suggestions presented here are general and can be adapted to fit specific camping situations.

Allow adequate time to create a group spirit among the camp counselors and leadership. Try to go beyond name, rank, and serial number to find out about life experiences, goals, and what each individual brings to the camp. Be creative and intentional. For instance, break into small groups and ask each person to describe his or her life as a youngster about the age of the campers. What was important? What activities were enjoyable? How were others viewed?

Melding counselors into leadership team members requires a full orientation to the mission and vision of the particular camp. Explaining the meaning and purpose behind your camp motivates the counselors to work together with leadership, campers, and one another to reach the camp's goal. Orientation should build familiarity with theme, slogan, music theme, and worship times, using the musical resources with which they need to familiarize themselves. Be sure to work through key curriculum experiences they will use with campers. Build community within the leadership team through a shared story time in which counselors describe their response to God and their faith at an age that is close to the camper's age. Use orientation session modules in which key staff enrich the counselor team with a Bible study, an inspirational sermon, or a commissioning sermon. The counselors will come on board for ministry as they grasp the sense of mission that drives the entire camp experience.

One year, the middle school camp Steve codirected chose the theme *HeartStrings*. We wanted to address relationships the campers had with family, friends, and God—those who hold a string to our hearts.

In addition to handing out curriculum packages to the counselors with stated overall and daily goals, the worship leader wrote a song called *HeartStrings* and taught it to the counselors and the campers. We sang our theme at every activity, and soon our hearts and our heads were feeling and thinking *HeartStrings*.

Familiarize the counseling staff with campground safety rules. An on-site manager may be available to speak to the counselors about safety procedures in the event of an emergency such as fire, severe storm, or flood. Also, address specific safety concerns and guidelines unique to that particular campground. These may relate to swimming, boating, adventure courses, area wildlife and plant life, or other aspects of the campground you are using.

If counselors are expected to work in pairs or groups, such as with small groups or in cabins, let these counselors get to know each other. Give them some time to share and pray together. Let them actually work through the camper response parts of the curriculum and distribute leadership responsibilities so the camper curriculum flows as naturally as breathing. Make it a rule that no camper is asked to share a story until a counselor has offered a personal story first—a story on which campers can build for style and emphasis. If, for example, counselors model honesty in response to invitations to share, campers will tend to share honestly.

Leadership team planning will distribute wide responsibility among counselors. They will volunteer or negotiate their "best gifts," which might include giving a morning devotional, leading a hike, singing a song or sharing a testimony during camp worship, helping with registration, assisting with games, praying before a Bible study, or participating in other planned activities. Empower the counselors as much as possible to be visible mentors and models for campers who are coming to admire them.

Do not neglect the issue of sexual integrity and sexual boundaries between counselors and counselors as well as between counselors and campers. The leadership team must define these integrity and boundary issues and must enforce guidelines that insure the safety of the campers as well as the integrity of the counselors. A counselor may hug a camper appropriately, or counselors may share an appropriate touch, but there are boundaries which are always honored (between campers also). Some issues to consider include:

- Absolutely no kissing or boyfriend-girlfriend relationships between campers and counselors. No games that play on kissing or "truth or dare" opportunities to embarrass campers by trivializing their most urgent present agenda: sexual privacy, the yearning for love, and expressing love in high-fidelity marriage.
- Male-to-male and female-to-female ministry and counseling is the rule for one-on-one situations. If private counseling is necessary, recruit a teenage peer to sit in on the consultation. This provides a remarkably safe "trinitarian" ministry base.
- No joking about the sexual history or experience of any camper, and no prying into it.
- No hugging, slapping, or other kinds of touching that could be interpreted as sexually inappropriate.
- Respect the campers' rights to limit even casual contact that violates personal boundaries, even though it is not of a sexual nature. Group huddles that include arm-to-shoulder touch are less offensive to males than holding hands, for example, so be sensitive to structuring contacts that are affirming to everyone.

Develop guidelines for dealing with camper reports of prior abuse and assist the counselors in working with that plan. Since laws vary by location, the camp leadership may have to do some research in this area in order to alert all staff to the legal and ethical guidelines that are required. The camp director should handle any cases of reported abuse. A standardized document may be prepared that includes:

- Name of counselor or other staff reporting abuse
- Name, age, sex, address, and phone number of the camper
- Date and time of initial conversation with camper
- Person named as having allegedly abused the camper
- Information regarding the relationship between the accused and the abused, for example, family member, neighbor, camp staff member or another relationship

- Record of victim's statement with regard to type(s) and date(s) of abuse
- Name and phone number of agency to whom the abuse was reported (enter date the report was filed)
- Name(s) of parents, pastor, or other persons informed of the alleged abuse, as directed by appropriate agency
- Name(s) of camp counselors, leadership and/or staff who were informed of or heard the camper speak about the alleged abuse
- Again, depending on area laws and specific policies, copies of the abuse report form may be confidentially filed with the campground, camp director, and other appropriate denominational or church officials, as necessary. The purpose of a mandated abuse report procedure is to insure the continued safety and protection of the campers, and to maintain responsibility among the camp leaders.

MORE RESOURCES TO HELP YOU FOLLOW UP WHAT YOU HAVE LEARNED FROM THIS CHAPTER

Cagle, Bob. *Youth Ministry Camping: A Start to Finish Guide to Helping Teenagers Experience the Greatness of God's Creation.* Loveland, Colo.: Group, 1989.

Chapter 10 has some good material, including ready-to-go events for counselor training.

Christian Camping International's Focus Series. Christian Camping International/USA, Box 646, Wheaton, Ill. 60189.

Several of the eight-page pamphlets in this series relate to camp counselors, including "The Counselor's Role in Camper Discipline,"; "How to Recruit and Encourage Volunteers,"; "Age Group Characteristics: Key to Understanding Kids,"; and "Camping and the Church."

Johnson, Becca Cowan. *For Their Sake: Recognizing, Responding to, and Reporting Child Abuse.* Martinsville, Ind.: American Camping Association, 1992. (A handbook for staff training by the same name was published in 1993.

Learn about identifying, responding to, and reporting possible child abuse.

Kalisch, Kenneth R. *The Role of the Instructor in the Outward Bound Educational Process.* Three Lakes, Wis.: Honey Rock Camp, Northwoods Campus, Wheaton College, 1979.

Though written from the Outward Bound perspective, this book contains helpful discussion of the camp counselor's role.

Sow Seeds, Trust the Promise. EcuFilm, 810 12th Ave. S., Nashville, TN 32703.

This four-part video series is about training outdoor ministry volunteers. Each part is thirty minutes in length.

7

RITES OF PASSAGE

It was getting dark as a light rain began to fall. We had finished our supper and some of the high school students were anxiously making preparations for bed. Our backpacking trip would end with just a few more miles hiking the next day. Although the campers were not aware of it, the leaders were preparing for a different experience.

The eight teenagers gathered their ponchos and were told to wait about one hundred yards away from the smoldering campfire. Then, one at a time, the four leaders brought one of the teenagers back to the fire. There he or she was asked formally and solemnly to assume the rights and freedoms of responsible adulthood.

The walking sticks on which they had carved secret symbols of past events were washed in a purifying bath. Each camper was given a gold nail cross on a leather thong, symbolizing personal acceptance of the way of the cross. Finally, when all the teenagers had been initiated, their pastor-mentor offered Holy Communion, sealing the ritual process to adulthood with a response of faith. From this day on the teenagers would be considered adult members of society by those present as well as by those at their home church.

DEFINING RITES OF PASSAGE

A rite of passage occurs when significant experienced members of the community preside over the initiation of less experienced members and welcome them to new, highly desired status, roles, responsibilities, and values. If the culture neglects rites of transition from childhood to adulthood, children will tend to attempt to initiate themselves which can lead to tragic manipulation of the young by mean-spirited peers.

Many traditional and tribal cultures observe rites of birth, childhood, adulthood, and death. The rituals clearly delineate the stages of life and mark endings and beginnings that the entire community or tribe can celebrate. There is no more powerful way of learning than to move in "ritual space." Peak experiences across a lifetime tend to combine significant changes in status, role, responsibility, and value—all marked by gesture, movement, and ceremony.

In a camp setting it is easy to create ritual space, a unique environment in which profound change and memorable learning can occur. A structured rite of passage encourages teens to accept adult responsibilities and gives them the support and understanding they need to help them accept the challenge of full adult freedom and responsibility.

In *Meeting the Tree of Life*, John Tallmadge describes a five-stage growth in awareness that comes from what he calls "reading the Book of Nature": (1) alienation and excitement of preparation, (2) pain of withdrawal, (3) fierce alertness of awakening, (4) poise and grace of encounter, and (5) bittersweet resolution of returning. These stages round out a transforming sequence of exposure to God's message in the natural order.

The hunger for ritual process seems to be universal, since children long to embrace adulthood. Traditional and tribal cultures have effective rites of passage that are composed of three distinct elements: (1) separation, (2) transition, and (3) reincorporation. First, the candidate is separated from normal routines connected with family, peers, and surroundings, everything that normally define a teen's role, status, value, and responsibility.

Second, candidates are brought to a liminal environment (in this case, to a camp setting) with others who have accepted the challenge to relinquish most of their usual childhood props. It is here that the real learning takes place: renegotiating and redefining who they are and who they want to be, what they must leave behind, and what reward they choose to embrace. Under the careful guidance of mentors and counselors, teenagers are instructed in adult ways and responsibilities and are given an opportunity to grasp them as their own.

Third, teens are reintroduced into their former environment and setting at a new, higher level. The old is gone and the new has come, and it is better than what they had imagined!

These elements can be illustrated in this fashion:

Figure 7.1
Rites of Passage

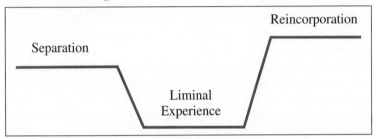

WHY RITES OF PASSAGE ARE NEEDED

Adolescence is a cultural invention that extends the period of time between childhood and adulthood. It serves as a holding tank for the young. It is a modern Western phenomenon that serves economic and social priorities valued by the culture.

Adolescence is defined as the period between puberty and economic and social independence. It is a time that is betwixt and between childhood and adulthood, which is dominated by feelings of alienation toward both. Today some want to push the age boundaries of adolescence to age forty. These persons consume destructive substances, sleep around but live alone, avoid adult responsibilities to lovers, to children, and to financial solvency. Adolescence may have become a cultural virus that infects many who are married with children, as at midlife they return to the indulgence pattern that society created for the teenage years.

A factor that has contributed to the rise of adolescence is the changing perception of puberty and the falling age of its onset. Strictly speaking, puberty marks a two-year period when fertility is developing and full height is being achieved. Puberty used to be thought of as the beginning of adulthood, but now it marks the beginning of a state of limbo between childhood and adulthood.

Puberty is occurring at earlier ages in North America and Western Europe. In 1840 the average age of first ovulation and menstruation was eighteen. By 1960 it had dropped to thirteen, and today it typically arrives *before* a girl's thirteenth birthday. First ejaculation of semen occurs twelve to eighteen months later than the onset of ovulation and menstruation.

For about three thousand years the minimum legal age for marriage was twelve years for women and fourteen years for men. Then, about one hundred years ago, just as the onset of puberty came earlier, the minimum legal age for marriage went up in the United States and Europe. Although teenagers had been treated as adults for thousands of years, they were now redefined as children. As these trend lines crossed, adolescence was created. While many people refer to adolescence as a period of temporary insanity between childhood and adulthood, it should be noted that it is our culture, not our teens, which is insane.

Rites of passage are missing from our culture but are present in most cultures that do not recognize this ten-year (or so) interlude between childhood and adulthood.

- In the Shin Byu ceremony, Buddhist children are transformed into adult Buddhists as they follow the Buddha's own transition from wealth to enlightenment.
- After his bar mitzvah (or after her bat mitzvah) a thirteen year-old child is recognized as an adult Jew.
- Through the kisungu rite, Basanga girls of Zaire are initiated into the world of adulthood through the symbolic death of their childhood.

No standard rite of passage from childhood to adulthood exists in North America. Instead, the lengthy and ill-defined state of adolescence prevails. Biological and psychological transitions take place unaided by the surrounding culture that could give them meaning and empowerment. Indeed, just when American teenagers need adults the most, in the years of their developing sexuality and cognitive decision-making abilities, our society leaves them to themselves with cries of "I don't understand you!"

USING RITES OF PASSAGE IN CAMPING

Rites of passage can be incorporated into a variety of camp settings. Simply attending a camp follows the broad outlines of a rite, including separation from home, transition into a new and temporary environment, and reincorporation into a new community as the camp experience climaxes and ends with the forging of new relationships. The goal is to highlight the elements of the camp experience that strengthen teenagers' resolve to progress to a higher level and to provide appropriate ritual experiences that can give the rite a lasting influence in their lives.

Varied elements of camp can be developed into a progressive set of rites for campers as peak experiences of resolve, determination and change become associated with ritual space and memory. A series of rites will serve our Christian formational goals well. Some of these rituals may focus on:

- celebrating the acquisition of a new skill, such as horseback riding, sailing, canoeing, outdoor cooking, or other camp-related activity,
- recognizing accomplishment and achievement such as finishing a challenge course, hiking to a certain landmark, performing at a new level in a sport, or helping another camper with a special emotional or physical need,
- discussing adult issues openly and frankly in terms of personal responsibility and hope for the future

The following guidelines are intended to help design a rite of passage for use at camp:

- Target youth who are approaching sexual maturity.
- Enlist counselors who can serve as mentors to the campers. Involve parents as presenters and witnesses, since empowerment through ritual process requires affirmation by unrelated mentors as "high priests" of the new status. The element of separation includes significant separation from parents and relatives.
- Inform participating churches and youth groups about the significance of camping and the rites experienced there so they can give public recognition to the candidates when they return home. This can help make reincorporation as meaningful as possible. Use counselors and leaders from churches as mentors for youth who came from those churches and will now return home at a new and higher level.
- Assist counselors and repeat campers in preparing first-time campers to anticipate what is to come and to celebrate with those who have journeyed through the established rites of passage into adulthood.
- Celebrate, celebrate, celebrate!

EXAMPLES OF RITES OF PASSAGE

The following rites of passage have been used in various camps and church settings. They can be modified to fit any religious camp. The first example was taken from a backpacking curriculum, *Path to Adulthood,* which was written for high school youth of Bovina, Texas, at the climax of a Rocky Mountain camping trip. The service was conducted the last night on the trail and was described in the illustration that opened this chapter.

Supplies needed:

1. Walking sticks and New Testaments for all participants

2. A nail cross on a leather cord for each participant
3. One sheet large enough to place over the shoulders of the candidates during initiation
4. Wash rag in a pot of water over a campfire
5. Copies of this rite of passage for all adults
6. Appropriate juice, cup and bread for Holy Communion

All the teenagers should be gathered together in one place, which is some distance from the site of the ceremony. The first five stations of the rite of passage are performed individually with each teenage backpacker. After all teenagers have been initiated, proceed with stations six and seven.

Station 1: Putting Away Childish Things

All adults should be wearing a gold nail cross. A parent/sponsor leads in a teen camper carrying walking stick and Bible and wearing the sheet draped over his or her shoulders.

Trip Leader: Who is this boy/girl? Why do you bring him/her here before these adults?

Parent/Sponsor: You are mistaken! This is no boy/girl! Sunday, when we left Bovina, he/she was but a child, but today I present to you and the others an adult who deserves all the freedoms and responsibilities that adults deserve.

Trip Leader (speaking to the teenager): What do you say? Are you a child or are you an adult?

Teenager: When I was a child, I talked like a child, I thought like a child, I reasoned like a child. When I became an adult, I put childish ways behind me (from 1 Cor 13:11 NIV).

Trip Leader: Have you done this? Have you put childish ways behind you?

Teenager: Yes, I have.

Trip Leader (to adults): What do you say? Is this a child or is this an adult?

Adults: We see no child before us. A few days ago, we were not sure, but today we know that [name of teen] is one of us. He/She is truly an adult, and we like what we see in him/her.

Station 2: Giving God Who I Am

The parent/sponsor now joins the other adults; the teenager is left with the trip leader.

Trip Leader: So, you are truly an adult, and we want to honor and respect you as one of us. What will you do with your new freedoms? Will you give God all that you are?

Teenager: Yes, I will. I have been crucified with Christ and I no longer live, but Christ lives in me. The life I live in the body, I live by faith in the Son of God, who loved me and gave himself for me (from Gal 2:20 NIV).

Trip Leader: (takes teenager's walking stick and washes it with water from a pot on the fire): Your life is purified and has been joined with Christ's. You are awesome in his sight.

Adults: We too give God our very lives and choose to live for him.

Station 3: Dealing with My Sin

Trip Leader: The good news of the gospel is that while we were still sinners, Christ died for us (from Rom 5:8 NIV). What do you say about the sin in your own life? What will you do with it?

Teenager: I count myself dead to sin but alive to God in Christ Jesus. Therefore I do not let sin reign in my body, nor will I obey its evil desires. I do not offer my body to sin as an instrument of wickedness but rather offer myself to God as one who has been brought from death to life; and I offer the parts of my body to him as instruments of righteousness. Sin shall not be my master because I live under God's grace (from Rom 6:11–14 NIV).

Trip Leader and Adults: In the name and authority of Jesus Christ, we pronounce that you are forgiven in Christ and offer you his peace for your life (from Jn 20:23 NIV).

Trip Leader: (removes sheet from camper): You are clean, you are a new creation (from 2 Cor 5:17 NIV)! You are set free from your sin to serve Jesus.

Station 4: Giving God Who I Am Becoming

Parent/Sponsor: I am proud of [name] and am thankful for the wise choices he/she has made, including his/her decision to present himself/herself to Jesus. I think [name] will continue to make wise decisions in the future, and I bless him/her and his/her future in the name of our Lord Jesus Christ.

Trip Leader: You've made it this far and now as an adult, with God's help, you can make it farther still. But I ask you, Will you give your future, your sexual energy, your marriage, your children, your job, your education, all that you hope to be—to Jesus this day?

Teenager: Not that I have already obtained all this, or have already been made perfect, but I press on to take hold of that for which Christ Jesus took hold of me. Friends, I do not consider myself yet to have taken hold of it. But one thing I do: Forgetting what is behind and straining toward what is ahead, I press on toward the goal to win the prize for which God has called me heavenward in Christ Jesus (from Phil 3:12–14 NIV).

Station 5: Receiving God's Call

Trip leader moves toward the teenager and puts a gold nail cross on a leather cord around his/her neck.

Trip Leader: Jesus has called you to serve and to live faithfully in God's will for you, honoring those around you and living always faithful to God. This nail cross lanyard is a symbol to remind you that following Jesus will not always be easy, but you will never be alone. Even when you feel God has left you, you will have many Christian brothers and sisters to lift you up. We will always love you and respect you. You have changed our lives. Seeing Jesus in you reminds us how much we love him too. (Appropriate affirmations, hugs, embraces.)

Now the teenager goes to stand with the adults.

Station 6: Following Jesus

After all the candidates have been initiated through station 5, proceed to stages 6 and 7.

Trip Leader: It will not always be easy, following Jesus. What will you do? How will you respond when the going gets difficult?

All Together: Praise be to the God and Father of our Lord Jesus Christ. In his great mercy he has given us new birth into a living hope through the resurrection of Jesus Christ from the dead, and into an inheritance that can never perish, spoil or fade—kept in heaven for you, who through faith are shielded by God's power until the coming of the salvation that is ready to be revealed in the last time. In this you greatly rejoice, though now for a little while you may have had to suffer grief in all kinds of trials. These have come so that your faith—of greater worth than gold, which perishes even though refined by fire—may be proved genuine and may result in praise, glory and honor when Jesus Christ is revealed. Though you have not seen him, you love him; and even though you do not see him now, you believe in him and are filled with an inexpressible and glorious joy, for you are receiving the goal of your faith, the salvation of your souls (from 1 Peter 1:3–9 NIV).

Trip Leader: The nails in our crosses remind us of the hardships of following Jesus. Our nail cross is gold, however, to remind us of how we are being changed and refined as Jesus walks with us through our trials.

Station 7: Holy Communion

Trip leader reads from Luke 22:19–22. After a prayer of consecration, all the backpackers come forward to take Communion.

Rite Initiating Adults in the Making

This next rite is adapted from a sexuality curriculum. It can be used at camp when the curriculum and theme have brought the campers to the door of adulthood through instruction and encouragement.

The students form a small circle in the center of the room (or outdoors, or wherever this rite will be used) facing out. The small group leaders then form a larger outer circle facing in. In this circle the leaders are facing their own campers if possible.

Campers in Unison: When I was a child, I talked like a child, I thought like a child, I reasoned like a child. Now that I'm maturing into an adult, I am putting childish ways behind me (from 1 Cor 13:11 NIV).

The campers now move into the outer circle with their small group leaders.

Small Group Leaders in Unison: We admit it. We think of you as children instead of "adults in the making." We celebrate your growth and maturity and the responsible decisions you have made. We commit you to the Lord of life and to the wise choices you have made to follow him. We know that "there is a time for everything, and a season for every activity under heaven: a time to be born and a time to die, a time to weep and a time to laugh, a time to mourn and a time to dance, a time to scatter stones and a time to gather them, a time to keep and a time to let go (from Eccles 3:1–6).

You have changed. You have matured. You will never be the same in our eyes again. In a wonderful way we are beginning to see you not as children but as our peers, and we are extremely happy.

Now the campers move out to form a wider, looser circle around the small group leaders. The group leaders now turn out to see their kids and the campers look in to see their leaders.

Small Group Leaders to Director (standing outside both circles): They know who they are and where they are going. They have made smart choices and responsible decisions. They may have some pain as they choose good in years to come, but even there, they are ready. I place them now in the care of the Lord Jesus Christ and this church. What will you say to them? How will you bless them? What gift do you bring them?

Director to Everyone: In the name of the Lord Jesus Christ and on behalf of this camp, I openly bless each of these campers. Today they are swinging between being children and being adults, between who their parents are and who they are, between heaven and hell. But I can see wisdom written on their faces and I stand with the angels and call them *blessed*. The gift I bring them is assurance that wherever they are in life, whoever they become, whatever questions, doubts, and suspicions they may have, they can *always* bring them to the adults with them now. We are big enough to bless their questions and honor their honest searching. We stand with these campers and among them as people who have brought our lives and the mysterious gift of our "image of God" sexuality and our relationships to Jesus. We sense that we too are still on this journey of obedience to Jesus and that the nails of the cross are symbols of our daily battle to be men and women of integrity. We welcome these new partners to the journey, knowing that God will be faithful to them too.

Here the camp director may pray a blessing on each candidate by name, joined by mentors or counselors, who lay hands on their shoulders or heads in final ritual process.

MORE RESOURCES TO HELP YOU FOLLOW UP WHAT YOU HAVE LEARNED FROM THIS CHAPTER

Joy, Donald M. *Empower Your Kids—To Be Adults! A Guide to Parents, Ministers, and Other Mentors*. Wilmore, Ky.: Center for the Study of the Family, 1998.
Reminds workers with youth in camping settings that Joseph Campbell was right. If we do not initiate our young into adulthood, they will try to initiate each other. Christian camping staff and volunteers often serve as officers of empowerment to emerging young adults who come to camp.

————. *Risk-Proofing Your Family*. Pasadena: U.S. Center for World Mission, 1993.
Seminal work on defining "adolescence" and the unprecedented challenge Western culture has invented for families. A foundational book to *Empower Your Kids*.

————. *Becoming a Man*. Ventura, Calif.: Regal, 1991; and *Celebrating the New Woman in the Family*. Anderson, Ind.: Bristol, 1993.
Books written for the author's teenage grandchildren—a grandfather's "rite of passage" gift to the third generation in the family.

Hill, Paul Jr. *Coming of Age: African American Male Rites-of-Passage.*
    Chicago: African American Images, 1992.
This subculture identity grounding program is a model for all of us
struggling to find strategies for grounding our families and children in a
faith community which is, by definition, the minority culture compared
to the dominant pagan culture.

Koteskey, Ronald L. "Adolescence as Cultural Invention," In *Handbook
    of Youth Ministry*, eds. Donald Ratcliff and James A. Davies. Birm-
    ingham, Ala.: Religious Education Press, 1991.
Offers research insights and alternatives to our culture's infatuation with
adolescence.

Schultze, Quentin, Roy M. Anker, James D. Bratt, William D. Roman-
    owski, John W. Worst, and Lambert Zuidervaart. *Dancing in the Dark:
    Youth, Popular Culture, and the Electronic Media.* Grand Rapids:
    Eerdmans, 1991.
This research team analyzes the shape of adolescence today and documents both its origins in our culture and its expansion to include people
at midlife who are abandoning adult responsibilities in search of a return
to the extravagance and irresponsibility of adolescence.

Tallmadge, John. *Meeting the Tree of Life.* Salt Lake City: University of
    Utah Press, 1997.
Useful in orienting camp volunteers and staff to the matchless sanctifying
power of reading the book of nature—God's creation exposed to us in
camping, regional parks, and wild reserves.

Venable, Stephen F. "Adolescent Rites of Passage: An Experiental
    Model." *Journal of Experiental Education* 20, no. 1 (1997): 6–13.
An examination of the significance of adolescent rites of passage with
helps for developing creative new ones to deliver the teens around you
from our culture's crucible of pain.

8

CREATIVE PROGRAMMING

Adolescence has become a holding tank in which we imprison our young to prevent their entry to the adult culture. Can we admit that we tend to pamper them with extravagant pleasures and programming and shield them from the challenging realities of the world? If so, perhaps they would benefit from attending a "ministry camp," which includes both high adventure and human service and caring?

This chapter shows how to design camp and work experiences that may be challenging but workable for some camping constituents. Accept the challenge to see camping as an opportunity to do ministry beyond the self-serving camp setting.

SPECIALTY CAMPS

Except for backpacking (see chap. 11), most of the material in this book relates to multiday residential camping experiences. That does not mean, however, that all residential camps have to be the same. One way to find focus and direction for a camp is to target a particular audience.

Camps for the Children of Divorced Parents

Recruit staff for the leadership team from your traditional camp. Families of divorce need an extra cadre of mentors and stable models for their children and youth. Gather emerging adults from families of divorce, along with other willing helpers, and plan to meet the special needs of these children and youth. A theme might focus on the steadfastness of God's love, putting the pieces back together, from many, one (especially for children now in blended families), finding hope. Let every activity, directly or indirectly, work toward the goal of reaching these children and youth with the message of the camp. Steve is familiar with a camp that is dedicated to children of divorce, Rainbow Camp. Special resources and training are needed for this effort, but they are available and the results justify the effort.

Camps for a Particular Ethnic Group

Another camp Steve is familiar with which also works well is Camp Amigos. It was started by an Anglo pastor and a Mexican-American pastor who wanted to see more Mexican-American children enjoying the benefits of camp. All summer camps scheduled by the sponsoring churches are open to children of all ethnic origins. And all camps are becoming increasingly rich in ethnic diversity. But both founding pastors agreed that Mexican-American campers deserved one summer camp that was dedicated to them and planned to meet their specific needs. For example, the camp is open to a wide range age-group so that siblings from a single family can attend together. Family is an important part of the culture. When a culture is not being reached by existing camps, it is a good idea to design one specifically for that culture to introduce the joys of camping to it.

Camps for Those with Physically or Mentally Handicapping Conditions

It is easy to recruit a leadership team from experienced campers. Several considerations must be taken into account: the age-group to be targeted, the level of handicap to be accepted, special training for staff, availability of local medical care, adapting the camp environment to facilitate the campers, and many, many more. More people are recognizing that persons with handicapping conditions deserve outdoor experiences with peers who are similarly challenged. Camping can be a great way to introduce them to the grace of a loving God.

Work Camps

Work camps are an important religious education tool to get youth directly involved in mission to those around them. In a work camp mentoring (see chap. 10) in a work camp can be easily arranged. It promotes informal discipleship as mature adult carpenters or medical specialists recruit and work alongside youth. Work camps, like other camps, vary in length, location, and emphasis, but they almost always provide an exceptionally powerful camp experience. Work camps are a matter of finding a house in your neighborhood or town that needs repair, gathering the necessary people and supplies, and going to work. Work camps can be held at other places such as a church-related campground, agency, or ministry that has some repair or building needs. There are several factors to take into consideration when planning a work camp.

1. Recruit the skilled workers necessary to do the work while mentoring inexperienced campers. Everyone must be able to sense making a positive contribution to the chosen task.
2. Recognize the fact that work camps offer an additional challenge. Campers must raise money for the time away as well as for materials needed to complete the work mission to which they travel. The entire work trip must be presented as a ministry mission. It will challenge the "extravagant consumption" and "fun" associated with traditional camping. Well-executed work missions consistently yield high rewards of deepened discipleship and maturity in the participants.
3. Start small with a weekend or local project and then build up to a more ambitious and distant one over time.
4. Invite people who have already participated in a work camp to speak to prospective campers to share the good news about what they contributed, and what they received.
5. Depending on the skills that the work projects require, specialized training might be necessary so all the participants can be ready to begin as soon as they arrive at the project site.
6. If traveling to an area with a different culture and language, spend some time studying the culture and the language to enhance contact with the residents on arrival.

7. During the work camp hold special sessions to debrief participants and reflect on the mission of the camp. The leadership
team will monitor the safety and well-being of their subgroups.
The process must be rich as the task is challenging. Be sure that
community building, recreation, and worship are daily "breathing exercises" in physical and spiritual wellness.

Adventure Camps

For example, a camp in Steve's region in west Texas, Ceta Canyon, is
situated in a canyon that is connected to nearby Palo Duro Canyon. In
addition to excellent cabin and programming facilities, camps in that
locality have been designed that enhance the campers' appreciation
of the outdoors and teach such skills as

- staying out overnight under the stars or in tents,
- fire building,
- cooking meals on a campfire,
- aanimal and plant identification,
- Indian lore regarding former residents of the canyon, and
- reflection on the wonder of God's created world.

Whatever resources are available in the local area, it is important
to plan a "not the same old" adventure camp.

Area of Need Camps

Identify an area of need for ministry and plan a camp around it. When
you identify a need, be sure that you have the people and resources
needed to address it. One popular ministry camp involves taking a
vacation Bible school to a missional area. Many churches have shifted
their vacation Bible school focus away from just reaching "their own"
children. They intentionally target a specific audience, such as the
unchurched or a particular ethnic group. It may be possible to cooperate with another church that lacks the volunteer or financial resources
necessary to offer an effective Bible school program. The sponsoring

church searches out a mission target and provides additional funding and materials and staff to conduct the religious camp or summer Bible school. Sometimes congregations prepare, staff, and equip a Bible school and "take it on the road" as a visiting Bible school to locations that otherwise would have no summer children's day camp or Bible school ministry.

To sum up, first, you need to know your group and what needs it is capable of meeting. Second, identify a church or church-related ministry that will benefit from what is available in your group. Third, work together to prepare your group to meet the targeted needs from the outside location. For example, a church-related ministry on an Indian reservation may be looking for a group to come and minister to local children through vacation Bible school, and you just happen to know some people with a heritage similar to the reservation residents'. The purpose of ministry will be accomplished when the resources you can identify match the expressed needs.

Specific Spiritual Need Camps

This type of camp will be as varied as the problems. Camps can be designed to

- teach about occult activity in your area;
- give youth workable alternatives to peer pressure relating to premarital sex, drug use, or alcohol abuse;
- create or enhance a spirit of community in a youth group that (for whatever reason) has no common bond;
- prepare high school graduates for the choices and responsibilities of the adult world;
- facilitate spiritual growth through traditional devotional methods from your own tradition. These might include (but are not limited to) prayer, reflection, solitude, Bible reading, community, and Holy Communion.

Dream a better world and then make that dream a reality.

CREATIVE PROGRAMMING
AT RESIDENTIAL CAMPS

Creative programming ideas can give new life to any traditional camp. The following are some helpful suggestions. It is important to adapt these suggestions to the specific goals of each camp.

Drama Workshop
Incorporate a hands-on drama workshop in place of a sit-down seminar. A drama workshop can be an exciting and compelling addition to a residential camp. The leader should be a facilitator/empowerer, not just a good performer. A good workshop requires a lot of advance preparation, such as gathering age-appropriate resources, recruiting additional workshop helpers, gathering necessary props or staging supplies, and so on. However, the rewards can be tremendous. Just as drama has a way of drawing the audience *into* the story on an emotional level, participating in a drama can be even more moving and transforming. Different drama formats include

- plays that tell a story related to the camp theme;
- acting out stories from the Bible;
- reenactments of real-life situations in which people's actions go against scriptural teaching;
- verba-mime, where participants silently "mime" a song as it is being played—a live music video.

The drama performances developed during these workshops can be performed by the campers during camp worship activities or at other appropriate times (see chap. 5). Also, it is often useful to make a videotape of the drama to help tell the camp's story throughout the year.

Missions
Make time to teach about or, better yet, participate in missions. Teenagers are becoming able to recognize and respond to the needs

of those around them. Though missions work takes on varied forms in different denominations, it universally calls on all Christians to look beyond themselves and actively take an interest in the lives of others. Missionary work is generally seen as a divine call, not simply a chosen profession. In this context campers can learn that all work can be sacred in nature.

As you contact missionaries and gather resources through your local church or denominational agency, look for the unexpected. Remember that much mission work is done locally, probably even in your community. Look for people or organizations in the local area that (1) serve the poor through distribution of food or clothing, (2) provide job training or housing, (3) focus their ministry to a particular ethnic population, or (4) reach out to a targeted audience such as youth or senior citizens.

Various types of agencies do mission work throughout the United States. These organizations may provide schools for the deaf, a temporary home for single pregnant women, a group home for orphaned or neglected children, an inner-city youth center, and so on.

Missionaries who travel abroad do far more than evangelize and establish churches. They help develop emerging farm crops, provide various medical services, establish schools, teach trades, and engage in many other activities.

Any mission group can come to camp and actively engage the campers in their particular purpose and vision. One year a couple who operate a maternity home and adoption agency came to the middle school camp Steve codirects. They shared the story of how they became involved in this ministry, described the training they received from the mission organization with which they were affiliated, and spoke about their work. They also addressed various issues relating to premarital sex, abstinence, and adoptive families.

Another possibility for service is doing work at the campground itself. Possible projects include clearing trails, painting walls, tearing down old buildings, marking nature trails, and so on. The goal is to get campers involved in missions, with their counselors and camp leaders right there with them.

Action Activities

Use action-oriented activities over sit-down seminars. Working within the camp's goals, set up a time that is just for fun. Call it Bible learning games, call it Crazy 'Lympics. Name it after your camp theme. Let your imagination go. Remember, these games should be noncompetitive, should involve everyone, and should be entirely safe.

Receive the Crown: Based on 1 Corinthians 9:25, "Everyone who competes in the games goes into strict training. They do it to get a crown that will not last; but we do it to get a crown that will last forever" (NIV). One person serves as coach and lines up the campers for exercises like jumping jacks, push-ups, and so on. The coach should tell the campers about the strict training regimen of the camp and about the prize to be won by all who follow the regimen. Finally, break into small groups. The counselors have lined up paper plates covered with shaving cream or nondairy topping, which they use to "crown" each member of the group. This can be followed by a discussion on what a life of faith requires.

Wandering in the Desert: This activity is based on the story of the Hebrew children wandering in the desert. Break into small groups and blindfold everybody except the designated leader. With everyone holding hands, the leader takes the group, by a roundabout route, to a particular spot at the campground, for example, the swimming pool, dining hall, or recreation center. The group members then guess where they are. Swap leaders, then go again. This can be followed by a discussion of direction and goals, especially in light of God's call on our lives.

Lean on Me: This game is from Ephesians 4:16, "From him the whole body, joined and held together by every supporting ligament, grows and builds itself up in love, as each part does its work" (NIV). Have pairs of youth face each other and stand just a little farther apart than their outstretched arms. With their palms turned up and their bodies straight, have them "fall" onto each other. When one catches the other by their palms, he or she says something positive and affirming about the person and then pushes him or her back upright. Then have the pairs move a little farther apart so that they are no longer able to catch each other. Next, have all the pairs line up shoulder to shoulder, still facing their partners, and have one line take a half-step to the right. Now the ones who fall will be staggered and held up by two people instead of one. One person on each end will need to use both hands to support one hand of the person opposite. People always say something positive about their partner(s) when they lean on them. Close this time with a discussion of what the game meant to the campers. Next read the Scripture and discuss the ways we all need each other.

INVOLVING THE ENTIRE CONGREGATION

Though everyone in the congregation may not attend camp, they can all participate at one level or another. Aside from enlisting youth to attend camp and recruiting adult members to serve as counselors, here are some other ways to involve as many people as possible:

- Find one or more people who will agree to pray for each person attending camp. These prayer partners will support and undergird the campers through prayer while they are away at camp.
- Invite the campers to earn some of the money to pay for camp through projects that serve the church or individual church members. Though some congregations budget a portion of each camper's expense, getting the campers and the congregation involved directly with each other may serve to strengthen and unify a church.
- Schedule a camp promotion day and ask senior members to talk about what camp was like when they attended years ago. Have them describe camp activities, and explain what the entire experience meant to them.
- When camp is over, invite the campers to share what the experience meant to them during an appropriate service at church. Be sure to invite the prayer partners to attend so they can hear for themselves how the life of the person they prayed for was changed.

MORE RESOURCES TO HELP YOU FOLLOW UP
WHAT YOU HAVE LEARNED FROM THIS CHAPTER

Hansen, Cindy S. *More . . . Group Retreats.* Loveland, Colo.: Group, 1987.

Plans for more than thirty creative, topical retreats.

Job, Rueben P. *A Journey toward Solitude and Community: A Guided Retreat in Spiritual Formation.* Nashville, Tenn.: The Upper Room, 1982.

Provides a great model for a camp or retreat that seeks a balance between solitude and community using classical disciplines.

Miller, Earl H. *Camping with Persons with Handicapping Conditions.* Nashville, Tenn.: Discipleship Resources, 1982.

Miller is a paraplegic pastor who tells of annual camps for disabled people, including information on staffing, training, program, health concerns, and so on.

Parolini, Stephen, and Lisa Baba Lauffer. *Fun Bible-Learning Projects for Young Teenagers.* Loveland, Colo.: Group, 1995.

Over one hundred projects, crafts, games, and activities, each teaching a message of faith.

Shaw, John C. *The Workcamp Experience: Involving Youth in Outreach to the Needy.* Loveland, Colo.: Group, 1987.

Written by a veteran in the field, this resource includes ideas on planning, budgeting, raising money, and a wide spectrum of organizational issues.

9

CHOICES AND STRATEGIES

Both authors have worked with traditional "flat-land" camps—camps chosen to accommodate family tents from the earliest days of camping in this century. There are church-owned state-of-the-art camp facilities that offer rugged terrain, rustic housing, wrangler and horsemanship training, and fine chapels on breathtaking vista points. Glory Ridge, near Asheville, North Carolina, was chosen by a visionary minister because it is the highest point in the area and suggests closeness to God. In this chapter we offer a checklist for developing the finest of residential religious camping experiences.

CHOOSING A CAMP SITE

Many camp directors have denominational campgrounds at their disposal. Other directors may face a scarcity of nearby facilities. Still other directors have a favorite camp that comes complete with friendly, permanent staff, and they return there year after year, thankful for the opportunity to do religious education camping ministry there.

A director who needs to select a site for the camp, however, needs to enter the process with much exploration, planning, and prayer. There are several questions that guide the site selection process.

Will the campground under consideration allow the program to adequately reach its goals? Make sure that the type and objectives of the camp can be achieved at any given camp. For instance, if nature awareness is a major goal, make sure the campground that is finally selected provides space and opportunity for ample contact with nature beyond the structures and improvements built at the campground.

What services are provided by the campground? Are meals provided? Is there a pool, lake, or beach for swimming? Is a lifeguard available? What other recreational opportunities are available? Is permanent staff available to instruct campers and counselors in safe enjoyment of the facilities? Will the group have exclusive use of the camp, or will other groups be present? Are the facilities adequate for the number of campers and counselors projected to participate?

What will it cost to use the facility? What is the cost per camper per meal? Are there additional fees for added services or personnel? Is there a price break after a certain number of campers? Do some cabins or lodges cost more than others?

Contact area pastors and youth ministers. Nothing is better than information from people who have already used a campground under consideration. Ask about everything from the condition of the bathrooms and beds to the quality of the food served to shelters and activities for a rainy day to the quality of the permanent staff. It is important to get direct description, not just a camp promotion package.

Make an on-site inspection. Go to the campground with a list of "must have" and "negotiable" features. Check everything out, even having a meal unannounced if possible. Get information on minimum and maximum group sizes, guidelines and rules for various facilities and activities, and information on how staff expertise in specific areas can be programmed into your camp experience. Once you have chosen a site, have an on-site planning retreat with camp leaders there. This is a great way to become personally acquainted with a new facility.

PRECAMP PLANNING

Establish Clear and Achievable Goals

Planning and preparation should wrap all aspects of the experience around the specific goals of the camp. Scheduling, crafts, worship, Bible studies, small group time, even meals and recreation time should help implement the established goals.

Write out the overall goals so that you know whether or not they are being achieved. Some possible goals for a worthwhile religious camp include

- introducing campers to God in a camp setting,
- providing an atmosphere of acceptance and grace in which all participants can discover God at work in their lives,
- meeting all campers where they are and respecting their own personal histories, experiences and humanity,
- providing campers an opportunity for greater commitment of their lives to God through the study of the Scriptures, bridging the gap between head and heart in faith and life in and through the campers in small group settings, and meaningful worship.

Choose an Appropriate Theme and Objectives That Are Designed to Meet the Goals

Everything flows from the camp's goals. Once the goals have been established, a particular theme, with its own set of objectives, can be properly aligned.

We have used the theme *HeartStrings* several times for a sixth- and seventh-grade five-day residential camp. *HeartStrings* refers to those who hold strings to the campers' hearts. The specific objectives of *HeartStrings* are for campers to

- experience an awareness of who they are from a biblical perspective of relationships with family, friends, and God;
- see themselves as unique persons who were created for love, not abuse;
- make lifelong commitment of their own unique abilities and life energies—their very selves—to the love and grace and understanding of God.

Budget with the Camper in Mind

Some planners start with a dollar amount: "We can only expect each camper to spend $____, so we'll plan accordingly." Others pick a campsite, select a theme, recruit outside talent for teaching, preaching, worship, music, and so on and then ask, "What's it going to cost each camper?" Regardless of how budget guidelines are established, it is essential to budget with the camper in mind. Religious camping is primarily designed to benefit the camper, not to bring attention and honor to the directors or other leaders.

The campground should charge a fixed fee per camper. Additional costs are covered by camper fees. The cost of honoraria or staff salaries must be collected from campers as well. Other costs include honoraria for key leaders, travel or other compensation for counselors and directors, additional food or snacks for staff, materials needed for scheduled activities such as Bible learning games and drama times, curriculum printing and supplies, publicity and counselor recruitment, telephone calls for coordination, planning, and recruiting, and craft supplies. There may also be other costs as well. Often district, conference, or regional religious organizations dedicate a "line item" to subsidizing the camp budget in order to keep camper registration fees low.

Schedule the Camp for Maximum Participation and Variety

Draw up a schedule that meets the goals of the camp and the theme objectives. The following schedule is only an example. It was designed with sixth- and seventh-grade campers in mind. A camp for high school youth might include more free time and no craft, for instance, while a camp for younger elementary kids might be more structured.

This schedule is for the middle three days of a five-day residential camp at an established campground with appropriate facilities and permanent staff. The first and last days are modified to fit changing arrival and departure times. (Registration begins around 2:00 p.m. on Monday; campers leave for home after the noon meal on Friday.)

- *Meals.* About fifteen minutes before each meal, some selected small groups may be needed to set tables and make other last-minute preparations in the dining hall.
- *Camp capers.* Small groups are assigned to clean certain areas of the camp each day. Depending on the number of groups and the size of the campground, some groups may not have to clean

Figure 9.1
Sample Camp Schedule

7:30	Rise and Shine
8:00–8:30	Breakfast
8:30–8:45	Camp capers
8:45–9:15	Devotions
9:15–10:15	Small group meeting
10:15–10:45	Snack bar
10:45–11:45	Bible learning games (BLG)
11:45 a.m.–12:30 p.m.	Bible study
12:30–1:30	Lunch and staff meeting
1:3–2:30	Rest in cabins
2:30–3:30	Missions/music/drama rotation
3:30–5:00	Snack bar
4:00–4:45	Swimming: Group A
	Recreation Time: Group B
4:45–5:30	Swimming: Group B
	Recreation Time: Group A
5:30–6:00	Get ready for supper
6:00–7:00	Supper
7:00–8:00	Small group meeting
8:15–9:15	Worship
9:15–9:45	Snack bar
9:45–10:15	Go to cabins and get ready for bed
10:15–10:30	Devotions in cabins
10:30 p.m.	LIGHTS OUT!

every day. The rotation is set up so that no small group has to do the same cleanup job more than once.

- *Devotions.* This is a campwide event that takes place in the tabernacle. Small groups sit together. Each morning counselors rotate the responsibility of sharing. It is a good idea to have some group singing before devotions start, if possible.
- *Small group meetings.* Small groups meet together in separate locations. They pick a spot, preferably outdoors, and meet there at small group time throughout the week. The camp curriculum should serve as a guide during these meeting times.
- *Snack bar.* Snack bars and vending machines are only available at certain times during the day.
- *Bible learning games (BLG).* More than anything else, this is a fun time. Junior counselors help codirectors run these activities, which are three games based loosely on Bible passages. One-third of the small groups rotate among each of the three games between Tuesday and Thursday. Leaders stay with their small groups at all times.
- *Bible study.* This changes from year to year and may be a drama, a dramatic reading, or a first-person presentation. It is usually done with the whole camp, sitting in small groups. The leaders tie the study into the curriculum material for each day.
- *Staff meeting/rest in cabins.* Campers are never left unattended. Half of the small group leaders come to a brief staff meeting while the other half stay with their small groups. The small group leaders attending the staff meeting can pass along necessary information to the others later.
- *Missions/music/drama rotation.* Over the years, this rotation has changed and shifted, but at present these three mediums are used to communicate the faith story and touch the campers' lives. One-third of the small groups rotate among each of these activities Tuesday through Thursday, using the Bible learning games rotation schedule.

Missions time gives the campers an opportunity to hear about a particular mission outreach or to participate in an actual work project

Figure 9.2
Sample Rotation Schedule

Location	Tuesday	Wednesday	Thursday
Tabernacle	Group A	Group B	Group C
Rec Pavilion	Group B	Group C	Group A
Dining Hall	Group C	Group A	Group B

at the campground. The music hour provides time for more personal interaction between the campers and the music leader. This time is used to teach the campers about the meaning of worship as well as the vital role that music plays. During the drama time each small group can develop a skit, a song, or a rap and then present it to the other small groups. A person skilled in drama can stir the campers' imaginations by starting this hour off with a specially prepared skit.

- *Swimming/recreation time*. Half of the camp swims while the other half is involved in one of several recreational opportunities. These opportunities will vary depending on what the campground has to offer.
- *Worship*. The entire camp assembles for worship, seated in small groups. The service includes group singing, perhaps a special song by a counselor or a camper, and a message from the camp preacher. Those who lead worship, such as worship leader, instrumentalist, preacher, and so forth, need to participate actively in the entire camping program. They should identify with campers as much as possible.
- *Devotions in cabins*. This activity helps the campers quiet down and go to bed. It is a time to find out what each camper experienced during the day. The focus of this activity should be on campers' needs and concerns.

Tell the Right People about the Camp

The goals and the theme of the camp must be established before the camp director can accurately communicate the expectations of the camp experience. Camp publicity should convey the theme of the camp, the camp target group, what age levels are included, dates of the camp, location of the camp, and costs to campers.

REGISTRATION

Every camp has a registration procedure. Forms and fees are distributed and sent through a church agency or conference jurisdiction for many directors. Other directors target their camp to one or a few churches or organizations.

Steve directs two kinds of camp each year. One is a five-day denominational residential camp at a conference-owned campground, which is attended by about three hundred campers and nearly eighty leaders. Registration is a major headache. Youth throughout the conference submit registration forms, which are first filtered through our conference center.

The other camp is a weeklong backpacking excursion sponsored by the church of which Steve is pastor. This camp is restricted to a total of twelve youth and adults. Registration poses no problems, since it consists of collecting signed medical release forms and money.

Preregistration

After a camper has been registered, a letter of confirmation should be sent that includes the beginning and ending times and dates, camper expectations, what to bring and what not to bring, and directions to the campground.

After the letter is sent, information is entered into a computer database. The database does not need to be an elaborate relational one. A simple flat-file database program serves well. If you do not have a computer, you can sort the forms by hand.

Figure 9.3
Sample Database Form

LASTNAME:	FIRSTNAME:
GRADE:	SEX:
CHURCH:	CITY:
ROOMMATE PREFERENCE #1:	
ROOMMATE PREFERENCE #2:	
ROOMMATE PREFERENCE #3:	
SMALL GROUP:	CABIN:

Once this information has been entered for all campers, separate listings can be made of male and female campers, sorted by church or city. SMALL GROUP and CABIN entries will be made later. Most roommate preferences cluster around the campers' home church, but this is not always the case. Thus care must be taken if preserving roommate preferences is a high priority.

Next, have one sheet of paper for each cabin, with lines or some indication of how many beds it has. You can now go down the printouts, placing campers by hand in cabins, remembering to leave enough beds open in each cabin for leaders. If possible, keep the number of small groups represented in each cabin as low as possible and make sure that cabin counselors have some (but not all) campers from their small groups in their cabins as well. When you enter counselors into the database, it is helpful to put COUNSELOR or some other code in the GRADE field to identify them.

To promote community building and bonding, avoid placing more than three friends together in cabin and small group assignments. After working out these assignments on paper, enter the data into the database. All camp participants can now be sorted by any field, so small group leaders, cabin counselors, directors, or permanent staff can know who should be where when.

The following is an easy way to inform preregistered campers of their cabin and small group assignments at the campground. Print a camp schedule for every camper and counselor. Then print mailing labels from your database, sorted alphabetically by LASTNAME, and separated by sex. The label can look something like this:

Figure 9.4
Sample Label

LASTNAME, FIRSTNAME
CHURCH   CITY
SMALL GROUP NAME
CABIN number OR NAME

Then attach the labels to the schedules, keeping them in alphabetical order and separated by gender. When registration begins, have the male campers come to one area that is grouped alphabetically (for example, A-E, F-J, H-L), and the female campers to another area. Counselors can then hand out the personalized schedules to the campers. Schedules that are not picked up are considered no-shows.

On-site Registration
On-site registration can be tricky, depending on the preregistration process. After the names of preregistered campers have been entered, a list of each cabin and small group can be generated that shows empty slots. These slots can be filled in during on-site registration, either on paper or on the computer. Each campground has a maximum number of campers which the registrar must adhere to. On-site campers should provide properly signed medical release forms and any registration fees.

Other Considerations
Be sure to give small group leaders a list of campers assigned to their group and cabin counselors a list of the campers in their cabin so at

the first small group meeting, or even when campers are checking into the cabins, they can be verified as having arrived at camp. No-shows should be reported to directors or a responsible party as soon as possible.

MORE RESOURCES TO HELP YOU FOLLOW UP WHAT YOU HAVE LEARNED FROM THIS CHAPTER

American Camping Association. *Camp Standards with Interpretations for the Accreditation of Organized Camps*. Martinsville, Ind.

————. *Occasional Papers*. Martinsville, Ind.
Camp Standards is a useful guideline for attaining excellence in planning and camp selection, while the *Occasional Papers* represent eight-page pamphlets on various camp themes. Contact ACA, Bradford Woods, 5000 State Rd. 67N., Martinsville, IN 46151-7902. (800/428-2267)

Cagle, Bob. *Youth Ministry Camping: A Start to Finish Guide to Helping Teenagers Experience the Greatness of God's Creation.* Loveland, Colo.: Group, 1989.
See especially chapters 2 and 5 for helpful suggestions for designing and carrying out a successful camp.

Kobielush, Bob. *How to Select the Right Camp or Conference*. Colorado Springs, Colo.: CCI/USA, Focus Series, 1995.

Pearson, John. *"Seven Steps for Effective Retreats."* Colorado Springs, Colo.: CCI/USA, Focus Series, 1995.
These two pamphlets are part of the *Focus Series* published by Christian Camping International/USA, Colorado Springs, Colorado. They are useful tools to use in making decisions about effective camp and retreat planning.

Goodrich, Lois. *Decentralized Camping*. Martinsville, Ind.: American Camping Association, 1982.
Goodrich's approach to camping will empower staff in forming small groups that develop community relationships and take responsibility for their own program and meals.

Van Matre, Steve. *Acclimatization*. Martinsville, Ind.: American Camping Association, 1972.
Van Matre offers strategies for putting campers in touch with the natural environment. There are also guidelines that help staff develop significant contact between campers and their world.

10

DEVELOPING A
LEADERSHIP TEAM

Lone ranger camp directors ride in out of nowhere and volunteer to recruit, staff, resource, and run a camp—often because no one else is willing to take the challenge and the need for a spiritually based camp is urgent.

In the summer of 1949, Don volunteered to direct a camp. Some intuitive sense drove him to search for colleagues with a similar passion. Within a few weeks six young adults with a vision for teenage camping in the High Plains convened for a leadership team. The Joy-Schufeldt-Hankins team laid the blueprint for Glory Haven Youth Camp, which operated for several years at a rental property near Lexington, Nebraska. The effectiveness of that camp for teenagers from western Kansas and Nebraska was remarkable. We pored over the design, hired a speaker, and distributed music, cooking, dietitian/food buying, and basic Bible teaching among ourselves and a few volunteers we recruited. Most of us also served as cabin counselors.

Don revisited that "leader team" concept as the Discipleship Development through Trail Camping course that was conducted summer after summer at Asbury Seminary. It was both a trail camp for teenagers and a training setting for youth ministers and pastors. In summer 1977, the Asbury seminarians became the leader team. Based on their April preregistration, they chose task force specializations in which to work as teams and organized the team according to gifts and skills. They analyzed the months between April and the camping trip, normally in early August. They used the program evaluation review technique to deal with the many converging schedules and tasks. More recently Don designed an advanced seminary course called Leadership Development through Program Planning to bring on board leaders with one season of trail camping behind them. With a leadership team Don becomes a facilitator, but the authority flows directly from the team members in both preparing and administering this remarkable teenage discipleship program. This combination of novice discipleship students being equipped by seasoned mentoring leaders has magic for designing, developing experience and content curricula, and mentoring the staff of novice graduate students in camp leadership training.

WHO ARE THE CAMP LEADERS?

Developing an effective camp leadership team is a real-life proposition, tested and tried in the crucible of shared lives, goals, and energies. Effective religious camp leaders do not sit in offices, surveying the campers and assigning jobs and responsibilities. Effective camp leaders bring together the campers, with their own peculiar set of needs and desires, and the volunteer counselors and advanced teen counselors in training. Leaders provide orientation. Leaders assess gifts and graces. Leaders articulate and nurture the camp's vision or purpose. The term "leadership team" refers to the people who design, equip and train, focus, and coordinate a camp experience. Effective leadership team members (1) are at camp for the campers, (2) lead by active participation, and (3) share leadership spontaneously with the team.

Are at Camp for the Campers

The leadership team at the annual sixth- and seventh-grade camp where Steve and his wife work is generally made up of six to eight adults coordinating the ministry of some seventy counselors in training who lead well over three hundred campers. Every year, the leadership team, as well as a governing camp commission, evaluates the effectiveness of the camp. Though gifts and graces vary across the team, their purpose is rock solid: to make a difference in the lives of young people. Possessing or exercising a particular gift or talent is not enough. Leadership team members use what they have for the sake of the campers.

Lead by Active Participation

It is not enough for ideas and plans to sound good or look good. Ideas and plans also must work. Through hands-on learning and training, leadership team members bring their training and experience to camp to creatively meet the campers' needs so that the goals of the camp are realized. Effective leaders learn by doing and are stimulated to greater learning by both their mistakes and their successes.

Share Leadership Spontaneously with the Team

Since effective leadership team members participate in camp for the sake of the campers and since they lead by active participation, they reflexively consult with the team when new challenges appear. Leadership teams who divide into tasks or spheres of specialization hammer out policy and make routine decisions that serve the camp mission. But lone rangers are dangerous. A team member who "shoots from the hip" can make decisions that compromise the mission or the morale of the camp. Leaders who mentor counselors in training and share responsibilities among a collegial camp administration team will replicate themselves for the future. They effectively transfer their experience to others through sharing leadership. Such collegial and mentoring leadership guarantees a continuing mission through their camp. Such shared leadership generates new leaders who will be even better equipped to lead since their own gifts blend with the experience of others. Perhaps a leader's greatest legacy lies in *who* that leader leaves behind, not *what*.

TRUE LEADERSHIP

The hallmark of leadership is authenticity, not power. To accept and to become who God has created us to be is an act of worship and an act of inner strength. True leadership originates out of the depths of this *being,* not simply in *doing*.

In her book *Real Power: Stages of Personal Power in Organizations*, author Janet Hagberg outlines six stages of personal power and relates each to various concepts and styles of leadership. For her, the external power to get things done flows directly from the inner power of personal identity. Hagberg's six stages are (1) powerlessness, (2) power by association, (3) power by symbols, (4) power by reflection, (5) power by purpose, and (6) power by gestalt.

Stage One
Those who are powerless tend to lead by force and inspire fear. If people at this stage are on the leadership team, they will need close monitoring. Stage 1 adults should lead youth or other adults. They are manipulators who can only watch out for themselves. Thus they are a real threat to the campers and do not comprehend the team leadership process.

Stage Two
People operating out of stage 2 are eager to use a leadership role to enhance a feeling of importance and power. They are likely to make decisions based on what serves their own desires. They tend to be overly dependent on the apparent chief executive officer (CEO). This "power by association" is a valid basis for being a protege, but the stage 2 person has not yet caught a glimpse of service through leadership—only a dream of being the CEO. Among counselors in training or even as junior members of a leadership team, stage 2 persons may catch a vision beyond themselves and become effective and mature leaders. But for now they are too narcissistic to operate without close mentoring by a senior staff member. The ego needs of stage 2 leaders get in the way of meeting young campers' needs.

Stage Three
Stage 3 leaders tend to be upwardly mobile and volunteer for any task or role that seems to have status value. They also tend to over-volunteer, to try to wear too many hats. For them, the symbol of title, visibility, and public recognition, or even popularity with the

camper audience is more important than the camp mission, camper needs, or the policies and procedures agreed on to provide a safe and effective camp. The energetic and often charismatic persons operating at stage 3 may attract personal followings and frequently are involved in minor conspiracies to abandon the camp mission or safety policies. Consequently these individuals often fail at the overall goal of their own personal transformation and growth and ministry for the benefit of all campers.

Stage Four
Leaders who are at stage 4 tend to be dedicated "to the death" to fulfillment of responsibility, fidelity to task, and protection of the campers. They model integrity and generate trust. They are visibly focused on "power by reflection," and this requires that they grow in self-knowledge and personal discipleship. Stage 4 leaders are not authoritarian. On the contrary, their ability to reflect allows them to learn from others. Leadership team members operating at stage 4 allow for diversity of opinion and style while instilling hope and trust among the campers and the other leaders, keeping the camp focused on mission and happy fulfillment of policy and procedures. Stage 4 leaders are excellent mentors for stage 2 novices, but they have little patience with the ego games of stage threes.

Stage Five
People at stage 5 are purposeful leaders who empower others. They are true servant leaders. These leaders see with more than their eyes and have a vision that extends beyond an activity or a project, even beyond camp itself. They give selflessly and are rewarded by seeing personal growth in others. Latch on to every stage 5 leader who can be found. They are more at home in a rustic cabin with twenty campers keeping them awake at night than sitting isolated in the staff cabin as the designated head honcho. Wherever they serve, those around them, young and old, prosper from their inner strength. Stage 5 leaders see value in all stages. They can understand the brittle punitive style of

a stage 1 who abuses power, and they make excellent mentors for stage 2 leaders. They are likely the best "lion tamers" for the unbridled ego appetites characterized by status-hungry stage 3 leaders. Stage 5 leaders (and stage 6 leaders) are most often people over forty and people who have suffered substantial pain or loss.

Stage Six
Leaders at stage 6, though rare, help build in others a deep sense of inner peace. They are the wise, the sages, the strong ones. By most standards they appear powerless, for they lead by wisdom, not symbols or positions of power. They are the perfect camp leaders, though they defy most conventional roles and expectations. They perform with abandon whatever job or responsibility they may have. But their primary work is helping others achieve purpose and meaning and peace in their lives. Be sure to recruit some senior partners to your leadership team who passionately support the mission of your camp and are committed to the coming generations of believing disciples of Jesus.

As you start to assemble a leadership team, look for the qualities of leadership in others. Then encourage them to lead! These necessary qualities are revealed in questions like the following:

- How can we commit more of ourselves to the campers, and what will be the result?
- What if we start from scratch and first ask, "What is the absolute best for the campers?"
- What is our long-term vision for the camp?
- How can we encourage the counselors to be creative and to give as much of themselves as possible?
- What if we trusted each other?
- Why don't we try it and see if it works?
- How can we strengthen one another?

PASSING ON WHAT HAS BEEN LEARNED

For true leadership to grow and continue, leaders must pass on to others what they have learned. In Hagberg's model, this begins at stage 4, when leaders reflect on who they are and where they have been. They begin to share their journey—themselves—with others. This process of passing on knowledge is often called skill- and self-mentoring. It is an age-old, though newly forgotten, art.

Elijah and Elisha

After he defeated the five hundred prophets of Baal on Mount Carmel (1 Kgs 18), Elijah fled to the desert because of Jezebel's death threat. He traveled on to Horeb, the mountain of God, where he heard God in a gentle whisper. There Elijah was given three specific instructions: to anoint Hazael king of Aram, to anoint Jehu king of Israel, and to anoint Elisha to succeed him as prophet.

> So Elijah went from there and found Elisha son of Shaphat. He was plowing with twelve yoke of oxen, and he himself was driving the twelfth pair. Elijah went up to him and threw his cloak around him. Elisha then left his oxen and ran after Elijah. "Let me kiss my father and mother good-by," he said, "and then I will come with you." . . . So Elisha left him and went back. He took his yoke of oxen and slaughtered them. He burned the plowing equipment to cook the meat and gave it to the people, and they ate. Then he set out to follow Elijah and became his attendant. (1 Kgs 19:19–21 NIV).

Soon Elijah would be carried away, and Elisha would inherit his ministry. But first Elisha learned from the crucible of life under the tutelage of his mentor, Elijah. This trial by fire was Elisha's anointing.

The Father, His Son and His Disciples

Jesus too was anointed to carry on God's ministry among his people. "The Spirit of the Lord is on me, because he has anointed me to preach good news to the poor" (Luke 4:18 NIV; compare Isaiah 61:1). Jesus quoted Isaiah 61 in the synagogue in his hometown of Nazareth to announce his role as God's protege. As Elisha was sent out by Elijah, Jesus was anointed to "go in his Father's place" and continue his ministry. In another equally telling passage Jesus went so far as to say that the "Son can do nothing by himself; he can do only what he sees his Father doing, because whatever the Father does the Son also does" (John 5:19 NIV).

After his resurrection Jesus similarly commissioned his disciples to continue in what he had taught and lived before them.

> Again Jesus said, "Peace be with you! As the Father has sent me, I am sending you." And with that he breathed on them and said, "Receive the Holy Spirit. If you forgive anyone his sins, they are forgiven; if you do not forgive them, they are not forgiven" (Jn 20:21–22 NIV).

The Holy Spirit, who had been present at Jesus' anointing (Lk 4), now carried his disciples into the next generation of the Father's work. Those who once followed were now called upon to lead.

Paul and Timothy

Another biblical example of the mentor/protege relationship is seen in Paul and Timothy. Paul's letters to Timothy reflect his love and affection for his protege: "To Timothy my true son in the faith" (1 Tim 1:2 NIV); "To Timothy, my dear son" (2 Tim 1:2 NIV).

Paul encouraged young Timothy "And the things you have heard me say in the presence of many faithful witnesses entrust to reliable men who will also be qualified to teach others" (2 Tim 2:2 NIV). This passage shows the continuity of the mentoring relationship, as the responsibility for passing on what has been learned continues as the protege becomes a mentor. The process repeats itself over and over again. Paul understood that mentoring is not something you return— you pass it on.

Levels of Mentoring

Mentoring relationships can have varying degrees of depth and breadth. Bob Shank describes three levels of mentoring, (1) role mentor, (2) soul mentor, and (3) whole mentor. The role mentor involves the centuries-old process of apprenticeship, in which the younger protege learns the skills necessary for a career from an older, experienced artisan. Today, role mentoring is less formal, but it is still popular for passing down skills and traditions.

The soul mentor level of mentoring can be described as finding spiritual direction. When two people give their full attention to what God is doing in their lives and seek to respond in faith, the work of spiritual direction is going on. At this level, a mentor may be known as a spiritual director. The ministry is perpetuated as the one seeking guidance eventually offers spiritual direction to another.

In the whole mentor relationship, whole lives become vulnerable to one another in an environment of mutual trust. Though proteges are generally perceived as being the open, growing ones in mentoring relationships, whole mentors recognize that their lives too must be totally open and approachable for their proteges to achieve maximum growth. Whole mentor relationships affirm the uniqueness and strengths of both pilgrimages.

PUTTING IT ALL TOGETHER

Perhaps the best term to summarize the desired qualities of a camp leadership team is *servant leadership*. Once again, Jesus is our model for true leadership. He did not lead by coercion or manipulation. Nor did he gain power through association with symbols of strength or with apparently influential people. Jesus' claim to leadership and to power are found in his chosen path of servanthood.

Jesus neared the end of his life on earth with an eye to what and who he would leave behind. Jesus knew

- what he had, "the Father had put all things under his power,"
- who he was, "he had come from God," and
- where he was going, "and was returning to God" (John 13:3 NIV).

Knowing all of this, Jesus had the strength to complete his vocation. He got up from supper and washed and dried everyone's feet. He took on the role of a servant.

> "Do you understand what I have done for you?" he asked them. "You call me 'Teacher' and 'Lord,' and rightly so, for that is what I am. Now that I, your Lord and Teacher, have washed your feet, you also should wash one another's feet. I have set an example that you should do as I have done for you. (John 13:12–15 NIV).

Turning every norm and expectation on its head, Jesus led his disciples from the heart. There are three characteristics of servant leadership to look for in assembling your camp leadership team. *First, servant leaders know their identity.* The leader who believes himself to be the all-important "big man at camp" barks commands and makes demands. But for the leader who knows herself to be someone commissioned to meet a goal—enhancing the spiritual lives of the campers—then no job is too big or too small if it achieves that objective. Cleaning latrines or handing out mail; resolving a conflict or soothing a homesick camper are one and the same. They all point back to what is best for the campers.

Second, servant leaders instill trust in one another. One of the reasons for assembling a leadership *team* is that no one person has to do everything. All people have different gifts. When the team comes together to plan or execute a camp experience, team members learn to trust each other's God-given graces. Servant leaders learn to let go of the need to have it their way. They allow one another space to carry out their camp responsibilities to the best of their abilities. Yes, there is interaction and discussion and flexibility. But there is also great trust in God's capacity to work in and through one another.

Third, and most of all, servant leaders serve. Servant leaders understand and live out the wisdom reflected in the prayer of St. Francis of Assisi:

O Divine Master, grant that I may not so much seek to be
consoled as to console; to be understood, as to understand;
to be loved, as to love. For it is in giving that we receive. It
is in pardoning that we are pardoned. And it is in dying that
we are born to eternal life.

MORE RESOURCES TO HELP YOU FOLLOW UP
WHAT YOU HAVE LEARNED FROM THIS CHAPTER

Biehl, Bobb. *Mentoring: Confidence in Finding a Mentor and Becoming
One*. Nashville: Broadman & Holman, 1996.

This is a valuable resource for anyone who wants to be a mentor to young
people today or for anyone who wants to find a mentor.

Engstrom, Ted W., with Norman B. Rohrer. *The Fine Art of Mentoring:
Passing On to Others What God Has Given to You.* Newburgh, Ind.:
Trinity, 1989.

A classic on mentoring. Engstrom shares the real-life experiences of those
who have been there and makes it work for everyone willing to learn.

Hagberg, Janet O. *Real Power: Stages of Personal Power in Organizations.* rev. ed. Salem, Wis.: Sheffield, 1994.

Hagberg's dissection and discussion of power is illuminating for its
reliance on the individual's inner self.

Joy, Donald M. *Following Close: A Mentor in Your Life.* Audiocassette.
Wilmore, Ky.: Center for the Family, 1995.

This personal and moving account of mentoring includes a helpful discussion of the components of mentoring relationships.

Peterson, Eugene H. *Working the Angles: The Shape of Pastoral Integrity.*
Grand Rapids: Eerdmans, 1987.

The subtitle should not fool the reader. This book is for all who are
committed to and interested in serving others.

Shank, Bob. *Enhancing Your Ministry Through Mentoring.* Audiotape
1660, vol 36. Pasadena, Calif.: Charles E. Fuller Institute, 1993.

A practical and thorough discussion of establishing and enhancing mentoring relationships as part of the camping ministry.

11

BACKPACKING

There is a growing interest in using off-site forms of camping, such as backpacking, to enhance campers' experience of God.

WHY BACKPACKING?

Backpacking can provide a very powerful experience that transforms campers deeply with the life-changing call of the gospel. Some have suggested that nothing we do offers greater potential for moral and spiritual development than wilderness camping. Bob Cagle calls back-packing an experiment in responsibility and Christian community. According to Cagle, backpacking challenges teenagers by fulfilling their urge for freedom and inviting them to test themselves beyond the boundaries of everyday life. The structure of the trail camp experience and the underlying matrix in which the entire backpacking experi-ence takes place constitute powerful "rails" on which this curriculum unfolds.

The structure of backcountry camping contains a fivefold analogy of the call to Christian commitment. First, backpack camping is de-signed as a journey, even a "pilgrimage" with ever unfolding agendas, challenges, even dangers. Second, backpacking reminds us that each day is tentative, that tomorrow will find us "at another place and time." Third, backpacking tests and refines the priorities and thins the "burden" to bare necessities, reminding us that survival is possible, even more probable, with a light load on your back. Fourth, trail camping inevitably revolves around emergencies and stresses that require "bearing one another burdens" as injury or illness shifts loads. Fifth, lifting the pack to get started again on the trail, helping tighten or loosen a belt or strap—these actions create a clear sense that we need each other more than we may care to admit. The words of Jesus on such issues form easily on the lips of campers who learn a rhythmic rap or chorus to set Scripture to a walking beat. "Jesus walked this lonesome valley. He had to walk it by himself! Oh, nobody else could walk it for him . . ." resonates with every adult and teen by the second or third day of the camp.

The living and breathing core matrix for backpack camping is, in a word, community. Community is also the common thread in residential camping, but in backpacking it is present at a deeper and even more powerful level. For most people, the wilderness is an unknown environment. This forces campers into a new dependence on God and each other. Further, backpacking forces us to leave behind even more of our props than does residential camping.

Community fills in the holes created by the missing props. Daryl Smith, veteran backpacker and Don's colleague at Asbury Seminary for many of the trips, outlines seven "community principles from the trail." They are all based on maintaining absolute respect—what he calls the *fleshing out* of love. These principles include: (1) community is basic; (2) cooperate, don't compete; (3) decisions are made by consensus; (4) community must be inclusive; (5) needs are shared openly, are respected, and are held in confidence; (6) trust God's Spirit in the community to change lives; (7) celebrate new life and keep the focus on Jesus.

GETTING STARTED

This chapter does not include an extensive treatment of backpacking, but it does provide a starting point for making initial plans and laying a groundwork for successful excursions into the wilderness.

Find an Experienced Trail Camp Leader

Of all the things a camp leader can learn from a book, the skills needed to take responsibility for a group of youth and adults in a wilderness environment are not among them. A trail camp leader must have experience in, for example, map reading, trail navigation, packing a backpack, campsite selection, outdoor cooking, equipment selection, maintenance and repair, wilderness emergency medical treatment, storm safety, and building a campfire. Most of all the backpacking leader must be willing to put the needs of the group above his or her own. It is a weighty feeling to have responsibility for a willing group of youth and adults alike many miles *by foot* from the nearest telephone.

All adults should be Red Cross certified in first aid and cardio-pulmonary resuscitation (CPR). The responsibility for the well-being of each backpacker should be taken seriously enough to contact your local Red Cross chapter to schedule available dates for training.

Locate Appropriate Backpacking Areas

Although far-off lands and distant locales are intriguing, there is a rewarding sense of ownership that comes from "living in" the land close to home. Organizations and resources such as the following can point the way to good backpacking areas:

- State and national parks, recreation areas, forests, and wilderness areas. The national headquarters of the forest service is: U.S. Forest Service, Department of Agriculture, 12th St. & Independence Ave., S. W., P. O. Box 96090, Washington, D.C. 20250, 202/447-3957.
- Local chapters of national wilderness organizations such as the Sierra Club. The national Sierra Club can be reached at Sierra Club Public Affairs, 730 Polk Street, San Francisco, CA 94109, 415/776-2211.
- Area or national print resources from a local bookstore. A section on areas of local interest will probably provide available books on area campsites and covering nearby hiking trails. Two books that provide national coverage are Charles Cook's *The Essential Guide to Hiking in the United States* and *The Essential Guide to Wilderness Camping/Backpacking in the United States.*

- Magazines related to outdoor adventure, such as *American Hiker, Backpacker, Outside,* or the more technical *Summit.*

Mapping the Trail

Once the backpacking area has been selected and good maps have been found, it is necessary to choose the particular trails to be traveled. Here are some criteria for selecting an appropriate route:

- Determine daily mileage minimums and maximums. Building community means leaving some slack, not pushing maximum mileage every day. The group may want to hike two days, take a day off, then hike two more days. This offers a good balance between the hard work of the trail and relaxation.
- A pilgrimage trail where everyone follows a single direction and moves toward a particular destination produces the best overall discipleship effects.
- Check with local forest service rangers or other authorities about possible changes along trails and to determine whether the trail that has been chosen is appropriate for the size of group. Also check on the current status of the water supply.
- Plan with emergencies in mind. Make notes on local access roads and possible evacuation points.
- Scout as much of the trail as possible. Make your way to the trail heads, even if you are not able to go over the entire trail.
- Print simple maps with a brief description of each day's hike for each camper. You can also have the trail scout brief the group every day.

Choosing the Right Equipment

As soon as word gets out that a camp leader wishes to take a group backpacking, friends and neighbors with supposedly solid gear stored in closets and attics will be beating a path to the leader's door, hoping he will take what they call "barely used" camping gear off their hands. Most of it will appear centuries old. The remainder might be good for typical tent camping, but it would fail miserably as appropriate backpacking gear.

A key feature in all good backpacking equipment is a balance between utility and weight. An old five-person green canvas tent with wooden poles and iron stakes might keep out the rain but its sheer weight and mass make it virtually impossible to pack up hill and down on the back of an ordinary human. Even ordinary necessities such as a flashlight can be pared down from a D-cell model to one that uses only two AA batteries.

When buying, renting, or borrowing equipment, keep the following hints in mind:

- Find nylon backpacks large enough to hold essentials but not big enough to invite overpacking. Avoid bags with any cotton content because they are heavy and they retain moisture. Though the debate over internal versus external frame packs drones on, they are approaching each other in utility and comfort. Find one that works for you. Always use a fully padded hip belt on each pack.
- Boots should offer lightweight support. Most major sneaker manufacturers now market one or more varieties of boots appropriate for the occasional backpacker. High-top basketball shoes work well, although they may not look like much by the end of the trip.
- Most nylon tents are not waterproof and require the use of an external, separate rain fly, almost always sold with the tent. A plastic or nylon ground cloth may be needed in addition to the floor of the tent. Make sure these pieces, as well as stakes, poles, and other necessary parts, are in good working order before leaving. Sometimes groups sleep under large tarps in trail families. While this can help promote group unity, it is also more vulnerable to the weather.
- Sleeping bags are not all alike. The bags that campers take should suit the climate and geography of the area where backpacking will occur. Bags are mummy (tapered at head and feet) or rectangular and are filled with down or a synthetic batting. Most sleeping bags

are temperature rated, but this figure is often a bit subjective, so be wary. A sleeping pad of some kind is a good idea to keep campers insulated from the ground and to smooth out rough terrain.

- Cook stoves should be lightweight yet powerful enough for the type of cooking and the number of people. Many areas restrict or prohibit fires or require additional permits for them to be built. "Low-impact" camping techniques stress the use of cook stoves to minimize stress and damage to the natural environment. The debate over fuel types (automobile gas, alcohol, butane, kerosene, propane, or white gas) can best be settled by buying the stove that fits the needs of the backpacking trip. Butane and propane cartridges add weight and cost, but they do not require pumping and may work better at lower temperatures. Do not hesitate with uninitiated campers to rely on van- or trailer-based traditional food service prepared over propane or gas stoves. When the benefits of trail camping as ministry are more of a priority than "doing it by the professional backpacker's book," the camp leader can use grocery store food and recruit some adult volunteers to coordinate the meal preparation at road-trail junction points throughout the trip.

- The cooking equipment should be large enough to be useful but light enough to carry if the leader is working with a dozen or fewer campers. The leader can form cook groups of about four, giving each group a standard cookset that includes a 1-quart pot, a 1½-quart pot, a 6-inch frying pan, and pot handles and pliers. Most meals only require normal knife, fork, and spoon utensils for preparation, which should be brought by each camper. All campers should also bring their own plate and cup.

- Some mail-order sources for quality gear include Campmor, P.O. Box 998, Paramus, NJ 07653, 800/226-7667 and REI (Recreation Equipment, Inc.), P.O. Box 88125, Seattle, WA 98138, 800/426-4840. Check out *Backpacker* magazine's annual gear guide for detailed information in summary form, published by Rodale Press, Inc., 33 E. Minor St., Emmaus, PA 18098, 800/666-3434.

Planning the Menu

Backpacking food is a mystery, even to seasoned backpackers. The balance between weight and utility helps decide what you eat. There are many lightweight freeze-dried packaged foods available, but they are also quite expensive. Plan well, shop around, and buy in bulk to repackage yourself when possible. Remember, anything that is not consumed must be packed out. Thus it is not wise to take food that is packaged in glass or in metal containers. Aluminum pouches can be packed out easily.

Here are some meal suggestions you can mix and match each day on the trail.

- Breakfast: prepackaged oatmeal (just add boiling water), pancakes (add water only), powdered eggs with bacon bits and/or squeeze cheese.
- Lunch: beef jerky, cheese and crackers, fruit rolls, summer sausage, dried fruit, peanut butter crackers, granola bars.
- Snack (in zip-lock bags): mix of peanuts (60 percent), dried fruit bits (20 percent), raisins (10 percent), chocolate or carob candy (10 percent).
- Dinner: lasagna, turkey tetrazzini, beef stew, chicken and rice, green beans, scalloped potatoes, corn, macaroni and cheese, fruit cobbler, cheese cake.

Only the dinner entrees, green beans, corn, and cobbler need to be bought as specialty freeze-dried items. All other items can be obtained at most grocery stores in plastic, paper, or aluminum packaging. For one-time campers from your church group, the volunteer chef can guide the preparation of fine meals from grocery store food.

Use a Theme That Fits the Natural Environment

The goals and objectives for growth and spiritual renewal through backpacking are best developed within the framework of the natural environment in which the trip will take place. In other words, do not take a group twelve hours from home and four miles from the nearest semblance of civilization so they can be told about the historical theology of one or another denomination. Discern a theme congruent with the God-created surroundings: mountain-top view, the ups and downs of the Christian life, winning over adversity. Or choose a theme that aligns psychologically with the stress of leaving home, being thrust into a new and sometimes hostile environment, and finally making it back home. Some ideas along this line include path to adulthood, growing up is hard to do, taking responsibility for who you are, choosing to live a life of faith, mountaintop, and other titles that serve as an umbrella for significant ritual and learning goals. (See chap. 7 on rites of passage for more information.) In addition to Bible study and sharing, it is helpful to provide each camper with a journal and pencil for daily reflection and writing. Questions for each day can relate to the curriculum or theme of the trip and some can be more general. Allow about thirty minutes of "solo" time each day on the trail so campers can be by themselves, enjoy their surroundings, and write in their journals.

HITTING THE TRAIL

What to Pack

The gear list will vary depending on climate, trip length, number of participants, how *rough* the trip will be, and a hundred other variables. Still, the following run-down can be a good starting place for deciding what to bring. Be sure to pack everything in large zip-lock bags to keep your supplies dry.

The first-aid kit carried by *each* backpacker should include at least band aids, gauze pads, moleskin for blisters, personal over-the-counter and/or prescription medicines (including ibuprofen or acetaminophen, antihistamines, antacids, and antidiarrhetics), elastic bandage, and antibiotic ointment.

Every group, though not necessarily every backpacker, should also carry additional supplies such as water purification tablets or filter,

Figure 11.1
What to Pack

CLOTHING		
Coat or jacket	Boots	Poncho
Socks	Shorts	Pants
Shirts	Underwear	Swimsuit
Bandanna	Gloves	Cap
PERSONAL GEAR		
Toilet paper (partial)	Toiletries	Sunglasses
Insect repellent	Sunscreen	Whistle lanyard
Small towel	1-qt. canteen	Extra zip-locks
Matches	Garbage bags	Small flashlight
Compass	Map	Camera
Fishing gear	Knife, fork, spoon	Plate
Nonmelting snacks	Tent	Sleeping bag
Sleeping pad	Backpack	First-aid kit

cook sets, stoves, and extra fuel. If poisonous snakes are native to the territory, it is important to train all campers to respond to a venom emergency. Traditional snakebite kits tend to bring about shock through loss of blood and are potentially more dangerous than snakebite.

The Ten Essentials

Every seasoned backpacker has a different response to the question, What do I *really* need to take backpacking? Over the years, a list of ten essential items has taken shape. Not all of these items need to be included in every backpack, but every group setting out on even a short day hike must have them all.

1. Map
2. Compass

3. Water

4. Extra food

5. Extra clothing

6. Matches

7. Fire starter

8. Flashlight with extra batteries

9. Knife

10. First-aid kit

A Word about Maps

A good topographical map of the trail may be hard to find, and learning to read one takes time and practice. Do not wait until the last minute to study the terrain. Study maps thoroughly before departing. A leader who does not know how to read maps well should get a good general book about backpacking and absorb the chapters on maps and compasses.

The maps need to provide detailed topographic information so that the leader can anticipate the terrain. It is also nice if the maps are printed on waterproof material. There are many sources for good maps.

- DeLorme Mapping publishes topographical maps of entire states. Many of the western and northeastern state books are in print. Contact them at DeLorme Mapping, Box 298, Freeport, ME 04032, 207/865-4171.
- Trails Illustrated prints maps based on U.S.G.S. topographical maps on a waterproof plastic material. You can reach them at Trails Illustrated, Box 3610, Evergreen, CO 80439-3425, 800/962-1643.
- The U.S. Geological Survey provides state-by-state indexes of topographic, geologic, and general maps. Contact them for an order form and a current list of maps at U.S.G.S. Map Sales, Box 25286, Denver, CO 80225, 800/USA-MAPS.

MORE RESOURCES TO HELP YOU FOLLOW UP
WHAT YOU HAVE LEARNED FROM THIS CHAPTER

Berger, Karen. *Hiking and Backpacking: A Complete Guide.* Trailside Series. New York: Norton, 1995.
A wonderful and colorful primer on the art of hiking and backpacking.

Douglas, David. *Wilderness Sojourn: Notes in the Desert Silence.* San Francisco, Calif.: Harper & Row, 1987.
A great Christian primer on the transforming power of the wilderness.

Hampton, Bruce, and David Cole. *Soft Paths: Revised and Updated.* Mechanicsburg, Pa.: Stackpole Books, 1995.
This is the National Outdoor Leadership School's leave no trace manifesto, covering almost every aspect of how to enjoy the wilderness without harming it.

Simmer, Peter, and John Sullivan. *The National Outdoor Leadership School's Wilderness Guide.* New York: Simon & Schuster, 1993.
This NOLS official wilderness camping guide is the ultimate reference book for responsible and effective use of backcountry camping as a curriculum and a learning environment. Updated, revised, and reissued edition.

Smith, Daryl. "Trailcamping: A Microcosm of Community." *Christian Education Journal* 10, no. 1 (1989): 51–62.
A solid theoretical grounding in the reality of the backpacking community.

Viehman, John, ed. *Trailside's Trail Food.* Trailside Series. Emmaus, Pa.: Rodale Press, 1993.
Includes good information on the types of food backpackers need as well as useful menus and preparation tips.

COMPETENT TO LEAD RELIGIOUS CAMPING: A QUICK SUMMARY OF WHAT YOU HAVE LEARNED FROM THIS BOOK

This chapter summarizes the ten principles behind religious camping that the authors have attempted to cover in the preceding chapters.

CAMPING AS AN ACTIVITY DEEPLY ROOTED IN BIBLICAL TRADITION

Beginning with the Exodus wilderness wanderings and continuing through the ministry of John the Baptist and even the temptation of Jesus, the Scriptures show God's transforming activity with humanity taking place outside the normal boundaries of place and routine. It is not just that Abraham and his descendants were nomadic people. God apparently chose such "campers" to more completely reveal himself, his purposes, and his ways. The incarnation found the divine nature of God separated from its true home. So campers too reenact the wilderness pilgrimage experience.

THE OVERWHELMING POWER OF COMMUNITY

Several factors play into the process of developing community at camps: time spent apart from everyday routines; the power of personal relationships that develop in small groups; the intensity of the time spent together in pursuit of the goals of the camp. Community is not something to be taken lightly. During the time set apart for camp, campers and counselors alike are searching for meaning and significance, and they often find it in the unique bonds that they form with one another. The experience of community at camp is magnified when the homes, communities, and churches we come from fail to reflect and make use of this strength.

BIBLE STUDY AS A TRANSFORMING TOOL

Camp Bible study is *not* an academic endeavor in an outdoor setting. It is an intentional and relational wrestling with the written account of humanity's quest for God. Religious camping has finding God as one of its overall goals (or at least the possibility of being found by God), and Scripture serves as a door through which we seek. People have been searching for God for millennia, and the Bible contains an account of that search. Through the study of the Scriptures, as well as through the natural setting of camp, persons seek to experience God.

WORSHIP AS A FOUNDATIONAL CAMP ACTIVITY IN WHICH WE RESPOND TO ALL THAT GOD HAS DONE FOR US

Worship involves a personal response to the relationship God offers to humanity, receiving God's mercy, re-ordering our lives around our relationship with God, and revealing God to others.

Camp employs various experiences to realize worship in new and meaningful ways, which open new doors for those who are willing to go through them. Through special meals, special places, and unique times during the camp experience, worship is recognized as a holistic and holy response to the God who reaches out to us in mercy and grace. Campers can participate in worship through singing, preaching, drama, and individual sharing. Worship at camp requires total involvement and vulnerability. It is not viewed as something some do while others look on.

CAMP COUNSELORS AS A KEY TO THE SUCCESS OF THE RELIGIOUS CAMP

Good camp counselors are born, not made. That may be overstating the case a little, but it remains true that the fundamental strengths of good camp counselors are more easily caught than taught. Counselors fill many roles, and potential counselors come from various backgrounds and age-groups. Some roles they are called on to play include spiritual compass and guide, facilitator/empowerer, responder, translator, and participant. Prospective counselors may be parents or grandparents, college students, or young adults. Even younger people—teenagers just a few years older than your campers—can serve as counselor trainees. It is critical that all camp counselors receive adequate training and orientation into their specific roles and responsibilities. Even though they are volunteers or relatives of campers, they must be fully aware of their responsibility both to the camp and to the legal obligations of counselors. The specific rules governing particular campgrounds need to be communicated to every counselor.

APPROPRIATE RITES OF PASSAGE AS EFFECTIVE TOOLS FOR TRANSFORMATION AND COMMITMENT

Rites of passage are culturally-recognized rituals that allow people of one group or age to move from their current level of responsibility to the next level. Rites allow for a clear distinction between each stage of life, and they provide the space to celebrate and embrace the significance of each step of progress achieved. Every viable rite of passage includes three elements: separation (campers are cut off from their normal, everyday routine); transition (campers are brought into their new environment with others who have similarly been separated from their usual routines); and reincorporation (campers go back to their old environments at a new and higher level of responsibility).

CREATIVE PROGRAMMING AS LOOKING BEYOND THE SAME OLD CAMP AND ENVISIONING NEW AVENUES FOR GROWTH

Camping programs, like other activities, can seek to re-create past successes instead of changing and adapting. Creative programming techniques attempt to re-think camp experiences, going back to the drawing board and asking: Will that activity *really* meet the desired objective in the lives of the campers? Aspects of creative camping include designing and implementing a specialty camp for a particular target audience, such as children of divorced parents, a particular ethnic group, or physically or mentally handicapped individuals. Creative programming views camp opportunities through new eyes: renegotiating primary objectives or environment, teaching and utilizing new skills, or targeting one very focused spiritual need, like helping high school seniors make responsible choices about their future. Creative programming is just that—creative.

IMPLEMENTING VARIOUS TYPES OF CAMPS, FROM PREPLANNING TO SCHEDULING TO BUDGETING

Precamp planning involves choosing a camp site, setting clear and achievable goals for your camp, discerning working objectives that support your goals, setting and staying within a reasonable budget, scheduling each day at camp for maximum participation and variety, communicating with the right people about your camp, and setting up the details of preregistration and on-site registration. Meals, worship, small groups, games, Bible studies, crafts, and a myriad of other issues must be planned and carried out in ways that meet the overall objectives of your camp.

DEVELOPING AN EFFECTIVE LEADERSHIP TEAM

Camp directors need to recruit a leadership team to join them in the ministry of camping. It is vital to recruit people who are committed to personal transformation and believe that others can be transformed through positive camping experiences. Some of these people enjoy participating in the full range of camping experience—as a leader and as a camper. Others include people who are at the camp for the campers, people who lead by participation and mentoring, and people who share the leadership mission and trust other members of the leader team. True leadership comes through integrity, not an authoritarian use of power. Leaders needed for a healthy camp environment lead by reflection, by empowering others, and by sharing their wisdom and inner peace with those around them. True leaders also pass on what they have learned to others. They use their gifts and graces to touch other leaders' lives, so a new generation can rise up and take on the continuing task of transformation through camping. These mentors guide their proteges to their maximum potential and instill in them a sense of servant leadership.

TRAIL CAMPING/BACKPACKING AS AN OUTDOOR LABORATORY FOR EXPERIENCING A CONCRETE MODEL OF CHRISTIAN DISCIPLESHIP—WALKING WITH JESUS, EVEN SUFFERING WITH JESUS

With the right leaders, trail camping and backpacking offer a dynamic opportunity for growth and strength. Backpackers are challenged to act on their urge for freedom and are invited to test themselves beyond the boundaries of everyday life. Backpacking offers an opportunity to experiment with responsibility and Christian community. The community developed on the trail can be a powerful tool for personal transformation. With the props of the everyday world left behind, a new dependence on God and each other can be fostered. Several steps for starting a backpacking ministry are outlined and include finding an experienced leader, determining an available backpacking site, mapping out an appropriate trail, choosing the right equipment, and planning the menu.

* *

Both of us, Steve and Don, thank you for walking with us through this manual. We expect to continue our camping ministry and leadership team development "so long as we have breath."

We would like to conclude this book by encouraging you to pay attention to Jesus. While the didactic "schooling" model of teaching was available to Jesus, complete with benches, tables, and writing surfaces, he rejected them and took his learners into the fields, to lake shores, and even across the Sea of Galilee. Jesus once observed that "foxes have holes, and birds of the air have nests, but the Son of Man has nowhere to lay his head" (Mt 8:20 NRSV). It is not likely that he was complaining but very likely that he was striking a profile of priorities. He went into the wilderness to accept the toughest spiritual battle he faced, and he habitually went to solitary outdoor places to pray. History began in the garden of Eden, passed through the garden of Gethsemane, and points to the celebration on the banks of the river of life. A deep and profound hunger for God persistently lures many of us away from the soft life and back into the countryside. Blessed camping!

INDEX

Abraham as a camper, 25, 115
abuse, reporting on, 55 f.
action programming, 78 f.
adolescence as cultural invention, 60 f., 70
adolescence, defined, 60 f.
adults, young, as counselors, 50
altar, response to God, 36
American Camping Association, 91
Americans, Native, and camping, 4
Anker, Roy M., 70
Ashram, Christian, 16

backpacking, 47, 104 ff.
backpacking, locating appropriate areas, 106 f.
backpacking, principles for, 105 f.
Balch, Ernest, 4–5
Bannerman, Glenn, 24
Baptist, John the, 6–7
bar mitzvah, as rite of passage, 61
Basanga girls of Zaire, ritual process, 61
Berger, Karen, 114
Bernice McCarthy, 27 ff., 35
Bible study, camping, 25
Bible study, transforming tool, 116
Biehl, Bobb, 103
bonding, in camping, 18
Bonhoeffer, Dietrich, 16, 24
Book of Nature, 59
boundaries, sexual, 54 f.
Bratt, James D., 70
budget for campers, 83

Cagle, Bob, 7, 10, 12, 14, 46, 56, 91, 104
camp registration, 88
camp schedule, example, 85
camp site selection, 81
Campfire Girls, 5
camping, back country, 104 ff.
camping, six dynamic principles, 9 ff.
camping, trail, 104 ff.
camping, wilderness, 104 ff.
camps, adventure, 74
camps, ethnic specialty 72
camps, for handicapping conditions, 72
camps, need based, 74 f.
camps, residential programming, 75 ff.
camps, specialty, 71 f.
camps, work, 72 ff.

Card, Michael, 8
challenge course, 23–24
children of divorced parents, 71 f.
Cole, David, 114
Coleman, Lyman, 24, 35
community, power of, 13, 115 ff.
conceptualization learning, 29
concrete learning, 29
congregational involvement, 779 f.
Cook, Charles, 106
cost, facility, 82
counselor trainees, 51
counselors, camp, 47 ff.
counselors, identifying potential and recruiting, 49
counselors, key to success at camp, 116
counselors, responsibilities of, defined, 51–52
counselors, training for, 52 ff.
course, ropes/challenge, 23–24
creative programming, for vital camping, 116

database, sample form, 89
Davies, James A., 70
decentralized program, 15 f.
delinquency, and camping, 8
desert, 6
diversity, required, 17
Douglas, David, 114
drama, and worship, 44
drama workshop, 76 f.

education, religious and holistic, 1
Eells, Eleanor, 3, 14
Elijah and Elisha as mentor and protégé, 99
Engstrom, Ted W., 103
equipment for trail camping, 107 ff.
ethnic specialty camps, 72
evangelism of campers, 52
Evans, Piromrak, 8
Exodus wilderness, 6, 115
experimentation learning, 29

facilitator/empowerer, counselor as, 48
Fakkema, Robert, 24
Father, Son, and disciples—empowering sequence, 99 f.
first aid, for backpacking, 111
Foster, Richard, 46
4-MAT System, 27 ff.
freedom and responsibility, 12

games, what to avoid, 55
goals and theme for campers, 83
goals, for site selection, 82
Goodrich, Lois, 11, 14, 17, 91
grandparents, as counselors, 50
Groome, Thomas, 30, 35
group building ideas and activities, 20 ff.
group, small-group guidelines, 18–19
groups, small, advantages of, 11
Gunn, Frederick William, 4

Hagberg, Janet, 95 ff., 103
Hampton, Bruce, 114
handicapping conditions camping, 72
Hannah, 25
Hansen, Cindy S., 80
health, spiritual, of campers, 52
Hill, Paul Jr., 70
Hinkley, George, 5
holy, as God is holy, 36

inspection, on-site, 82

Jesus, central to Christian camping, 18
Jesus, walking with, evening suffering with, 119 f.
Job, Rueben, P., 80
John the Baptist, 6–7, 115
Johnson, Becca Dowan, 56
Jones, E. Stanley, 16
Joy, Donald, 69, 103
Joy-Schufeldt-Hankins team, 93
Jung, Carl, 27

Kalisch, Kenneth R., 57
Kay, Linda, 8
kisungu ritual, 61
Kobielush, Bob, 91
koinonia, as community, 13, 16 ff.
Kolb, David, 27 ff.
Koteskey, Ronald L., 70

label, sample, 90
Lakeview Camp, 36
Lauffer, Lisa Baba, 80
leader development, 93 ff.
leadership team, 53 ff.
leadership team, development of, 93 ff., 119
leadership vs. performing, 41–42
leadership, qualities of, 98

121

122   Index